Everyone Loses:
The Ukraine Crisis and the Ruinous Contest for Post-Soviet Eurasia

Samuel Charap

Timothy J. Colton

IISS The International Institute for Strategic Studies

The International Institute for Strategic Studies

Arundel House | 13–15 Arundel Street | Temple Place | London | WC2R 3DX | UK

First published January 2017 **Routledge**
4 Park Square, Milton Park, Abingdon, Oxon, OX14 4RN

for **The International Institute for Strategic Studies**
Arundel House, 13–15 Arundel Street, Temple Place, London, WC2R 3DX, UK
www.iiss.org

Simultaneously published in the USA and Canada by **Routledge**
711 Third Ave., New York, NY 10017

Routledge is an imprint of Taylor & Francis, an Informa Business

© 2017 The International Institute for Strategic Studies

DIRECTOR-GENERAL AND CHIEF EXECUTIVE Dr John Chipman
EDITOR Dr Nicholas Redman
EDITORIAL Alice Aveson, Jill Lally, Carolyn West
COVER/PRODUCTION John Buck, Kelly Verity

The International Institute for Strategic Studies is an independent centre for research, information and debate on the problems of conflict, however caused, that have, or potentially have, an important military content. The Council and Staff of the Institute are international and its membership is drawn from almost 100 countries. The Institute is independent and it alone decides what activities to conduct. It owes no allegiance to any government, any group of governments or any political or other organisation. The IISS stresses rigorous research with a forward-looking policy orientation and places particular emphasis on bringing new perspectives to the strategic debate.

The Institute's publications are designed to meet the needs of a wider audience than its own membership and are available on subscription, by mail order and in good bookshops. Further details at www.iiss.org.

British Library Cataloguing in Publication Data
A catalogue record for this book is available from the British Library

Library of Congress Cataloging in Publication Data

ADELPHI series
ISSN 1944-5571

ADELPHI 460
ISBN 978-1-138-63308-7

Printed and bound by CPI Group (UK) Ltd, Croydon, CR0 4YY

Contents

ACKNOWLEDGEMENTS

The International Institute for Strategic Studies has been a nurturing and collegial professional environment for one of us (Charap) during the course of the research and writing. His co-author (Colton) has benefited greatly from the support of the Davis Center for Russian and Eurasian Studies and the Weatherhead Center for International Affairs, both at Harvard University, and from the Institut für die Wissenschaften vom Menschen, Vienna.

A number of colleagues in several countries were kind enough to read the draft and to supply thoughtful feedback: Steedman Hinckley, Sergei Karaganov, Ivan Krastev, Andrej Krickovic, Fyodor Lukyanov, Roderic Lyne, Neil MacFarlane, Michael McFaul, Alex Pravda, Mary Sarotte, Mikhail Troitskiy and Alexandra Vacroux, who was also a terrific organisational bulwark. The final product was greatly improved as a result, although, needless to say, responsibility for it is ours alone.

John Drennan of the IISS provided yeoman research assistance for the project from its early stages through the final throes. Without his sharp eye and unflappable determination, this book would not have been possible. IISS interns Valeria Bondareva and Tetyana Sydorenko also assisted with the research, under John's supervision. Neil Buckley of the *Financial Times* generously shared unpublished reporting materials from his files. We are grateful to Nicholas Redman at the IISS for commissioning this as an *Adelphi* book, for his patience throughout, and for giving the draft manuscript a careful review. We warmly thank Alice Aveson for her thorough copy edit, John Buck and Kelly Verity for the design of the cover and the graphics, and Gaynor Roberts for managing the editorial process. The Working Group on the Future of US–Russia Relations (supported by Carnegie Corporation of New York), while not directly involved with the book, supplied a discussion forum for many of the phenomena and ideas treated in *Everyone Loses*.

Finally, we are grateful to our spouses for tolerating a demanding writing schedule, particularly in the final months.

GLOSSARY

A/CFE	Agreement on Adaptation of the Treaty on Conventional Armed Forces in Europe
AA	Association Agreement
CFE	Treaty on Conventional Armed Forces in Europe
CIS	Commonwealth of Independent States
COMECON	Council for Mutual Economic Assistance
CSCE	Conference on Security and Co-operation in Europe
CSTO	Collective Security Treaty Organization
DCFTA	Deep and Comprehensive Free Trade Area agreement
DNR	Donetsk People's Republic
EC	European Community
EEC	Eurasian Economic Commission
EEU	Eurasian Economic Union
ENP	European Neighbourhood Policy
EU	European Union
GDR	German Democratic Republic
GTEP	Georgia Train and Equip Program
GUAM	Georgia, Ukraine, Azerbaijan and Moldova
GUUAM	Georgia, Ukraine, Uzbekistan, Azerbaijan and Moldova
IMF	International Monetary Fund
LNR	Luhansk People's Republic
MAP	Membership Action Plan
NATO	North Atlantic Treaty Organization
NGO	Non-governmental organisation
OHCHR	Office of the United Nations High Commissioner for Human Rights
OSCE	Organization for Security and Co-operation in Europe
PCA	Partnership and Cooperation Agreement
PfP	Partnership for Peace
PKF	Peacekeeping force
RSFSR	Russian Soviet Federative Socialist Republic
SES	Single Economic Space
USSR	Union of Soviet Socialist Republics, or Soviet Union
WTO	World Trade Organization

15 March 1988	Mikhail Gorbachev repudiates Brezhnev Doctrine justifying Soviet dominance over East Central Europe
9 November 1989	Fall of Berlin Wall
3 October 1990	Unification of East and West Germany
19 November 1990	CFE and Charter of Paris for a New Europe signed at CSCE
28 June 1991	COMECON disbanded
1 July 1991	Warsaw Pact disbanded
21 August 1991	Estonia, Latvia and Lithuania declare independence from USSR
8 December 1991	Belavezha Accords signed, declaring end of USSR and establishment of CIS
25 December 1991	Gorbachev resigns as president of Soviet Union
26 December 1991	Official dissolution of Soviet Union
15 May 1992	Collective Security Treaty (Tashkent Treaty) signed by Russia, Armenia, Kazakhstan, Kyrgyzstan, Tajikistan and Uzbekistan
24 June 1992	Moscow brokers end to war between Georgians and South Ossetians
21 July 1992	Ceasefire to end conflict in Moldova's Transnistria province
21–22 June 1993	Three Copenhagen Criteria for enlargement of the EU adopted at European Council in Copenhagen
10 January 1994	NATO PfP programme launched
14 May 1994	Moscow brokers end to war between Georgians and Abkhaz
5 December 1994	Budapest Memorandum on Security Assurances for Ukraine signed by Russia, US and UK
1 January 1995	CSCE renamed OSCE

27 May 1997	NATO–Russia Founding Act on Mutual Relations, Cooperation and Security signed
31 May 1997	Friendship treaty signed by Russian president Boris Yeltsin and Ukrainian president Leonid Kuchma
10 October 1997	Georgia, Ukraine, Azerbaijan and Moldova form GUAM consultative forum
12 March 1999	Czech Republic, Hungary and Poland join NATO
19 November 1999	A/CFE signed at Istanbul summit of OSCE
31 December 1999	Yeltsin resigns, Vladimir Putin becomes acting president of Russia
26 March 2000	Putin elected president
7 October 2002	Establishment of CSTO
23 November 2003	Eduard Shevardnadze resigns as Georgian president, in the culminating moment of Rose Revolution
24 November 2003	President Vladimir Voronin of Moldova scuttles 'Kozak Memorandum' plan for resolving the Transnistria dispute.
29 March 2004	Bulgaria, Estonia, Latvia, Lithuania, Romania, Slovakia and Slovenia join NATO
1 May 2004	Czech Republic, Estonia, Hungary, Latvia, Lithuania, Poland, Slovakia and Slovenia join EU
12 May 2004	European Neighbourhood Policy announced
28 December 2004	Viktor Yushchenko elected president of Ukraine in run-off prompted by Orange Revolution protests
3 April 2005	Tulip Revolution in Kyrgyzstan forces resignation of president Askar Akaev
10 May 2005	Russia and EU sign framework documents for four 'Common Spaces'
31 December 2005	First Russia–Ukraine gas war begins
12 December 2007	Putin suspends implementation of CFE agreement
2 March 2008	Dmitry Medvedev elected president of Russia
2–4 April 2008	NATO Bucharest summit communiqué declares Georgia and Ukraine 'will become' members of Alliance
5 June 2008	Medvedev calls for new European security treaty
8–12 August 2008	Russia–Georgia war
26 August 2008	Russia recognises independence of Abkhazia and South Ossetia

31 December 2008	Second Russia–Ukraine gas war begins
7 May 2009	Launch of EU Eastern Partnership initiative
9 June 2009	Russia, Kazakhstan and Belarus announce formation of Customs Union
29 November 2009	Russia publishes draft European Security Treaty
25 February 2010	Viktor Yanukovych elected president of Ukraine
15 April 2010	President Kurmanbek Bakiev ousted in Kyrgyzstan
21 April 2010	Yanukovych signs 25-year extension of lease on Russian Black Sea Fleet base in Crimea in return for discounted gas price
31 May 2010	Russia and EU launch Partnership for Modernization
20 November 2010	NATO–Russia Council agrees to 'work towards achieving a true strategic and modernised partnership' at Lisbon summit
4 March 2012	Putin elected to third term as president of Russia
30 March 2012	Ukraine and EU initial AA
3 September 2013	President Serzh Sargsyan announces Armenia will scrap AA and join EEU
21 November 2013	Ukrainian government suspends preparations for AA with EU
28–29 November 2013	At EU Eastern Partnership summit in Vilnius, Yanukovych refuses to sign AA despite intense pressure from EU leaders
30 November 2013	Police crack down on students demonstrating in Kyiv against decision not to sign AA
17 December 2013	Putin promises US$15bn in credits to Ukraine and cut in the gas price by one-third
18–20 February 2014	Dozens of protesters and police killed in bloodiest days of the Maidan Revolution
21 February 2014	Yanukovych and three opposition leaders sign agreement calling for government of national unity, constitutional reform and new presidential election
22 February 2014	Yanukovych flees Kyiv; Verkhovna Rada votes to remove him from office
25–28 February 2014	Russian reinforcements arrive in Crimea and fan out across the peninsula

1 March 2014	Putin obtains formal approval from upper house of parliament to deploy military forces on Ukrainian territory
15 March 2014	Russian Foreign Minister Sergei Lavrov presents US Secretary of State John Kerry with draft 'Friends of Ukraine' action plan
16 March 2014	Contested plebiscite held in Crimea; overwhelming majority of voters said to support unification with Russia
17 March 2014	US and EU enact sanctions against Russia
18 March 2014	Putin delivers blistering speech denouncing Western foreign policy and announcing the 'reunification' of Crimea with Russia
15 April 2014	Ukrainian government launches 'anti-terrorist operation' against Russia-backed anti-Maidan protesters who had taken up arms and seized administrative buildings in southern and eastern Ukraine
25 May 2014	Petro Poroshenko elected president of Ukraine
27 June 2014	Georgia, Moldova and Ukraine sign AAs with EU
16 July 2014	US Treasury Department implements sanctions on Russia's financial, defence and energy sectors
17 July 2014	Downing of Malaysia Airlines passenger jet over the Donbas
7 August 2014	Russia retaliates against sanctions with bans on imports of agricultural goods and foodstuffs
2 September 2014	Separatist counter-offensive, backed by Russia, ends in major Ukrainian defeat at Ilovaisk
5 September 2014	Representatives of Ukraine, Russia, the DNR and LNR sign ceasefire in Minsk, Belarus ('Minsk I')
1 January 2015	EEU launched
14 January–20 February 2015	Second Russian direct military intervention ends in capture of Debaltseve
12 February 2015	Angela Merkel, François Hollande, Putin and Poroshenko agree on second peace plan ('Minsk II')
12 August 2015	Kyrgyzstan joins EEU
21 December 2015	Russia–Ukraine–EU trade talks break down in acrimony
1 January 2016	Ukrainian DCFTA goes into effect; Russia suspends CIS trade preferences for Ukraine in retaliation

ABOUT THE AUTHORS

Samuel Charap is Senior Fellow for Russia and Eurasia at the International Institute for Strategic Studies, based in the Institute's Washington DC office. Prior to joining the Institute, Samuel served as Senior Advisor to the US Under Secretary of State for Arms Control and International Security, and on the Secretary of State's Policy Planning Staff.

Timothy J. Colton is Morris and Anna Feldberg Professor of Government and Russian Studies, Harvard University. He is a specialist on Russian and Eurasian politics and the author of *Yeltsin: A Life* (Basic Books, 2008), *Russia: What Everyone Needs to Know* (Oxford University Press, 2016) and other works. He is a Fellow of the American Academy of Arts and Sciences.

Note on transliteration

We use conventional transliterations of Russian and Ukrainian proper names that commonly appear in English (e.g., Yuri, Yulia, Moscow, Yeltsin). Ukrainian surnames and place names are transliterated from Ukrainian (so Kyiv, not Kiev). Citations are transliterated using the British Standard/*Oxford Guide to Style* system, with the exception of English-language references, which are not altered.

Map 1: **Cold War military alliances, 1989**

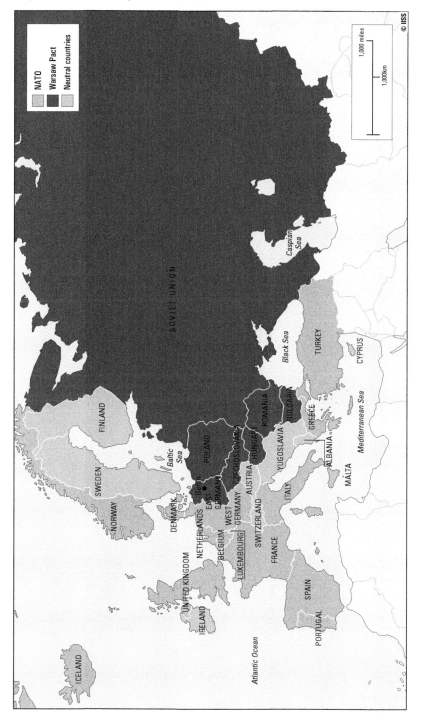

Map 2: **Military alliances and economic blocs, 2016**

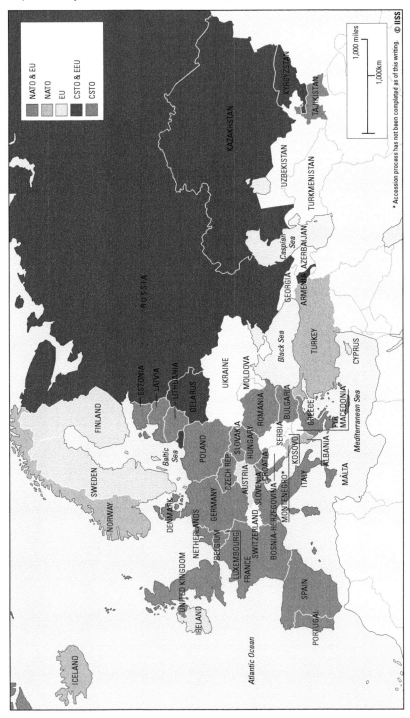

Map 3: **East Central Europe and Post-Soviet Eurasia**

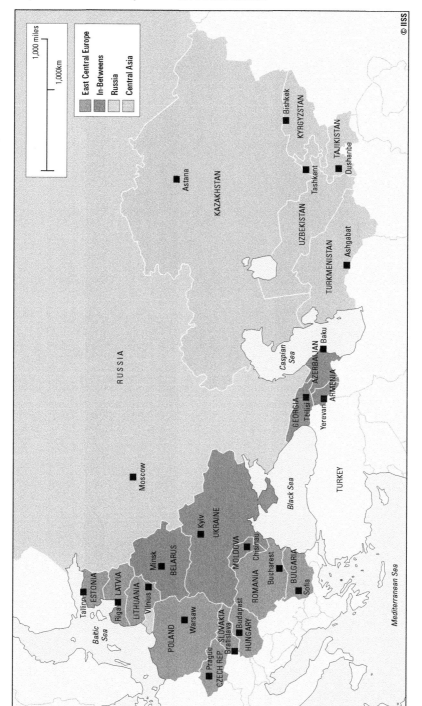

Map 4: **Separatist-controlled territory in eastern Ukraine, November 2016**

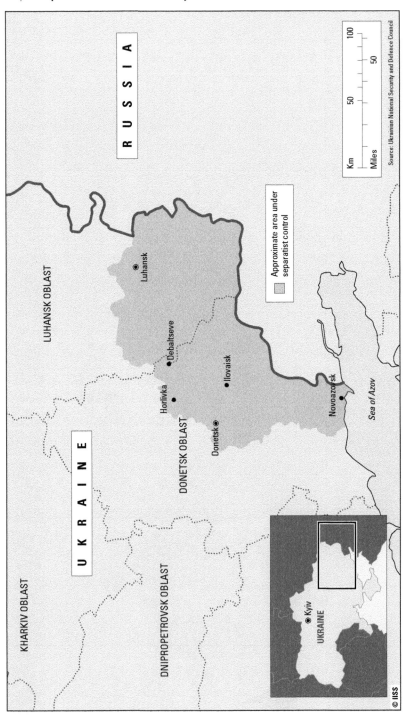

Western readers of the morning's headlines in 2014 realised to their surprise and dismay that post-Cold War Europe was at war. The local conflagrations triggered by the break-up of the Soviet Union and Yugoslavia in the 1990s were bloodier, but the Ukraine crisis occurred long afterwards and revived fears of a clash between major world powers. The United States and the member states of the European Union (EU) adopted positions diametrically opposed to those followed by post-Soviet Russia. Ukraine and its people were caught in between. Today, Europe is divided once again, although the divisions lie farther east than they did before the fall of the Berlin Wall. These new demarcation lines are unstable and reflect neither local affinities nor great-power consensus. There is talk in world capitals of a new cold war, a protracted period of tensions when destabilising and even catastrophic conflict is an ever-present danger.

The troubles in Ukraine began as an essentially internal affair. In November 2013 a crackdown on students demonstrating against the government's decision not to sign an agreement to link the country more closely with the EU led to a mammoth street protest in the capital city, Kyiv. Several months of clashes between the authorities and the protesters produced, unexpectedly for all, the violent overthrow in February 2014 of a harsh and erratic but democratically elected president, Viktor Yanukovych, in what came to be known as the Maidan Revolution. The domestic imbroglio blew up into an international confrontation in March when Russian President Vladimir Putin ordered measures taken to occupy and then annex the Crimean peninsula, situated on Ukraine's Black Sea coast.

While the Crimea operation produced few casualties, thousands have died since Moscow supported unrest in the Donbas area of eastern Ukraine, along the land border with Russia. Consisting of the provinces of Donetsk (pre-conflict population 4.4 million) and Luhansk (2.2m), the Donbas hosted a high concentration of the country's mining and metallurgy and was the political base of Yanukovych and his Party of Regions. Separatist 'people's republics', with material and moral support from Russia, were declared in both pieces of the Donbas in April 2014. A Ukrainian military operation to quell the rebellion began that spring and within months had forced a rebel retreat. Late that summer, regular Russian units – far better equipped and trained than their Donbas separatist comrades – intervened directly. The resulting setback for Ukrainian forces produced negotiations that led to a ceasefire deal, signed in Minsk, Belarus, on 5 September. It broke down within weeks. A second and more robust pact was signed on 12 February 2015, again in Minsk, following another punishing Russian intervention.

The crumbling of the first of the two Minsk agreements resulted in large part from the battle for control of the airport of the city of Donetsk, the provincial capital. This event serves as a powerful reminder of the destructive forces at work. Located ten kilometres northwest of central Donetsk, the facility was officially called Sergei Prokofiev International Airport, in honour of the world-renowned composer, a native of Donetsk province. Prokofiev was born there when it was part of the Russian Empire in the late nineteenth century, but lived and worked from 1936 until his death in 1953 in the USSR, specifically in what is now Russia.[1] While he identified as an ethnic Russian, Prokofiev inserted into his works motifs from the Ukrainian folk songs he had heard as a child. The airfield, first constructed by Soviet engineers in the 1940s, was renovated at great cost in 2011–12 as part of the preparations for the European football championship of 2012, co-hosted by Ukraine and Poland. Shiny and modern, the passenger terminal seemed to reflect the relative prosperity the Ukrainian industrial heartland had come to enjoy, as well as the country's increased international standing.

On 26 May 2014, insurgents loyal to the self-proclaimed Donetsk People's Republic (DNR) seized the airport. By the next evening, the Ukrainian military and pro-government militias had wrested back control. In the months that followed, they used the now-inoperative airport as a base to shell Donetsk city, the rebel stronghold. Accordingly, separatist forces began in late September to try to reverse their earlier defeat. In stages, this monument to inter-ethnic cooperation and the promise of globalisation was demolished. One by one, the air-traffic control tower, the new and old terminals, hangars, fuel-storage tanks, equipment sheds and a hotel were reduced to rubble or to charred hulks. The facility finally fell to the separatists in January 2015, by which time it looked like Second World War-era Stalingrad and was littered with broken glass, booby traps and burned-out vehicles. Sporadic fighting has continued around the defunct airport.

The tragedy of the grinding siege of the Sergei Prokofiev International Airport is that around 700 human beings died over a superfluous asset. The DNR had no air force, and in any event artillery rendered the runways useless during the first round of fighting. Ukrainian ground forces could have fired at the city, if they had so wished, from more readily defensible wooded areas nearby. The September truce had called for the airport to be ceded to the rebels. But Ukrainian soldiers remained encamped there in violation of the terms. They stayed because the glare of the television cameras made retreat to safety politically unattractive for their commanders and the leadership in Kyiv. On national television, these troops were lionised as 'cyborgs', super-human fighting machines prepared to battle to the death, as if the airport were a latter-day Alamo. Unlike the Alamo in Texas, however, this site had no military value to speak of. And, unlike the Mexicans who besieged the Alamo in 1836, the rebels here allowed the Ukrainian defenders to rotate in and out for several months, subject to inspection.[2]

The wrecked airport serves as an apt symbol for the gestalt we observe in the Ukraine crisis. Game theorists classify the result of a dispute or negotiation in one of three main categories. In a zero-sum game, one party gains from the interaction and the other correspondingly loses, with the respective winnings and losses adding up to zero. Hypothetical illustrations would be a competition between two unemployed persons over a single desirable job, or between two passengers in a sinking yacht over the one available life raft. In a positive-sum game, both actors benefit. For instance, negotiations over shares in a fixed pie of resources could produce insights into how to enlarge the pie so that both parties get more valuable slices than before, or the yacht passengers could find a way to activate a second life raft so that both of them survive. In a negative-sum interaction, by contrast, the pie or pool of available benefits shrinks, because of contextual changes or choices made by the parties involved, and each of them ends up worse off at the end of the day. In the theory of games, negative-sum interactions are appreciated as the ones that will generate the most severe discomfort and discord as the players work their way through them.

In our estimation, the best metaphor for the conflict in and over Ukraine is that of the negative-sum game, a ruinous scenario in which every major player loses.[3]

As far as Ukraine is concerned, its overall condition has degraded markedly since the crisis erupted in 2014. No one can be sure exactly how many Ukrainians have died in the fighting in the Donbas. The United Nations Office for the Coordination of Humanitarian Affairs puts the toll at about 10,000 as of August 2016. Almost 3m people have been forced from their homes. Much of the Donbas's vaunted stock of mines and industrial assets has been destroyed. Countless dwellings in the towns and cities of the region have been razed or smashed by indiscriminate shelling, as have electricity, water, sewage and other utilities.

Nationwide, the country has a new president (Petro Poroshenko, elected in May 2014) and a new parliament (elected in October 2014). But politics have become radicalised, and the state has been weakened, including by loss to volunteer paramilitary battalions of its monopoly over the use of force. The authorities are committed rhetorically to economic and political reform; results have been dilatory and quarrels over policy and patronage have abounded. Ukraine did sign the agreement with the EU that Yanukovych put on ice in 2013, but any pay-offs lie well in the future and there is no possibility of Ukraine becoming a full member of the bloc for many years to come, if ever. Ukrainian GDP slid by 7% in 2014 and another 10% in 2015, and that is counting production in areas no longer controlled by the central government.

The other actors in the ongoing saga have suffered less, but are certainly worse off than they were before the crisis began. Russia has gained some territory, true, but has paid dearly in economic terms and in international standing. The war footing and Western sanctions have weakened liberal impulses and strengthened conformist pressures within the polity while adding to the hyper-personalisation of political life around Putin. The economic downturn that has ensued, while not an exclusive result of Ukraine-related turbulence and Western sanctions (falling oil prices have been more debilitating), has only made things worse. Russia shows no inclination to annex the Donbas but has had to shell out tens of billions of roubles to ease its misery. Crimea, now de facto incorporated into the Russian state, will burden the treasury in the coming years, and Western sanctions and cut-offs in trade with and supply of irrigation water and electric power from the Ukrainian mainland have made life difficult for inhabitants of the peninsula.

The EU and the US, while less acutely affected, have not come out unscathed. For Europe, the crisis is possibly a direct threat to its security and is a very real, and very costly, policy quagmire. The EU's Eastern Partnership, of which the agreement with Ukraine is an integral component, was intended to create a band of stable and prosperous countries along the Union's borders. Ukraine, the largest neighbour, is today anything but stable and prosperous, and the EU has felt compelled to sink billions of euros into keeping it afloat. The sanctions and Russian counter-sanctions have hit European economies at a time when they can ill afford it. And the Ukraine gas-transit corridor is under perpetual threat of shut-off, jeopardising much of the broader EU–Russia gas trade. Washington for its part has felt required to bolster deployments and military expenditures in Europe in the context of tight budgets and competing demands from the 'pivot' toward the Asia-Pacific and the turmoil in the Middle East. The complete breakdown in US–Russia relations, which were bad to begin with, stands in the way of efforts to address all manner of global challenges.

In sum, the Ukraine crisis has catalysed a negative-sum political interaction. All of the parties to it, in our view, are worse off than before it began.

The central claim of this book is that the negative-sum outcome we behold today is a product of zero-sum policies pursued by Russia, the US and the EU. These developed fitfully in the first decade and a half after the Cold War but dramatically intensified thereafter. Russia and the West implemented policies toward the states of post-Soviet Eurasia that aimed to extract gains at the other side's expense, without regard for overlapping or shared interests. Neither invested serious effort in the task of outlining or even contemplating a cooperative regional order that all parties could accept. The result has been not only a deepening east–west divide, but also dysfunction in the politics of the region's states, where elites seek to milk this contestation to suit their own narrow, often pecuniary, interests.

Analysis done in the midst of a crisis generally tends to shed more heat than light. Much of what has been said and written about the Ukraine crisis is no exception. The roots of the crisis extend far beyond the political earthquake in Kyiv and Russia's jarring response. This volume seeks to understand those events as an outcome of the recent, post-Soviet past. Its purpose is analytical, not normative. We do not seek to assign blame or to provide justification for any party's actions, not only because making such judgements is not our role but also because no party to this chain of events has clean hands. Indeed, this book will demonstrate that constructive, considered policy and actions in this region were the exception, not the norm, for all sides.

Several alternative explanations of the Ukraine crisis – and particularly of Russia's actions – have emerged since the watershed of early 2014.[4] The most prominent describes the crisis as a result of Russia's nefarious ambitions toward its neighbours. Through this optic, Moscow harbours the long-term strategic objective of subjugating all former Soviet lands. The latest manifestation of this strategy is said to be the Eurasian Economic Union (EEU), a Moscow-led regional economic-integration bloc, which Russia purportedly sought to compel Ukraine to join. As Serhy Yekelchyk writes, 'The [Maidan Revolution] frustrated Russia's political leaders, who had just forced the Yanukovych regime to turn its back on the West. The Kremlin could not undo the overthrow of its ally in Kyiv, but it could cripple the new Ukraine while at the same time asserting Russia's greater geopolitical role.'[5] According to Andrew Wilson, it was 'Russia's addiction to dangerous myths', including 'that the former USSR was the "lost territory" of historical Russia', that explains the annexation of Crimea and the intervention in eastern Ukraine that followed.[6]

It should astonish no one that a country of Russia's capabilities and ambitions will seek influence over its periphery; the US or China are no different in that respect. And it is clear that early in Yanukovych's presidency Russia wanted to bring him around to joining the EEU, and between late 2013 and early 2014 wielded sticks and carrots to keep Ukraine from signing an Association Agreement (AA) with the EU. But to begin and end our understanding of the Ukraine crisis with Moscow's supposed grand strategy of regional hegemony assumes that Russian actions in Ukraine in 2014 (and in the broader region) occurred in a vacuum, which, as this book will demonstrate, is contrary to the record.

The converse argument – that the Ukraine crisis resulted primarily from the West's policies toward the region – has been made by several prominent international-relations scholars of the realist school, as well as some Russia experts. Writing in *Foreign Affairs*, John Mearsheimer posited that 'Washington may not like Moscow's position, but it should understand the logic behind it. This is Geopolitics 101: great powers are always sensitive to potential threats near their home territory.'[7] The threat, he and others have argued, was a Western intent to bring Ukraine into the North Atlantic Treaty Organization (NATO) and shatter Russia's position there, a plan that accelerated toward implementation with the Maidan Revolution. The West, says Andrei Tsygankov, 'made Russia's conflict with Ukraine possible, even inevitable', by not recognising 'Russia's values and interests in Eurasia'.[8] Yet just as Russian policies were not formulated in a vacuum, neither were Western ones; without examining their dynamic interaction (the 'game') we cannot gain full purchase on the Ukraine crisis. Moreover, to decry Western policy as deliberately hostile and portray Russian actions as having a 'rational and empirical basis', as Richard Sakwa does, obscures that interaction almost completely.[9]

Other explanations have turned the lens from the international level to the domestic. The events of 2014, accordingly, are said to have flowed from changes inside the perpetrator, Russia, and the Kremlin's response to them. As Michael McFaul and Kathryn Stoner-Weiss write, 'Russia's foreign policy, including specifically the annexation of Crimea and military intervention in Eastern Ukraine, did not change in response to [Western policy]. Rather, Russian foreign policy changed in large measure as a result of Putin's response to new domestic political and economic challenges inside Russia.'[10] Specifically, Putin's approval ratings slackened following the flawed 2011–12 election cycle, there were street protests in Russian cities in that period, and economic growth slowed, casting doubt on the previous social contract. The Kremlin decided to fashion a new contract based on protecting the Russian people from external threats. 'To maintain his argument for legitimacy at home, Putin needs perpetual conflict with external enemies.'[11]

To be sure, the Ukraine crisis provided a domestic political windfall for Putin; his approval ratings hit stratospheric highs after the annexation of Crimea, peaking at nearly 90%. But we should be wary of confusing cause and effect. By the time Yanukovych's government fell, Putin had effectively addressed the challenges of 2011–12. He had squelched organised opposition through targeted repression; opened new release valves for discontent through measures like a return to gubernatorial elections; and reinforced the loyalty of his coterie through a drive for 'nationalisation of the elite'. In other words, as the Maidan Revolution unfolded in Ukraine, Putin faced no serious threat to his rule in the short to medium term, enjoying prodigious popular support and elite fealty. It seems far-fetched that under these circumstances he would have taken so disruptive and risky a set of actions purely in order to prop himself up politically at home.

Rajan Menon and Eugene Rumer, in *Conflict in Ukraine: The Unwinding of the Post-Cold War Order*, rightly point our attention to the regional context. They argue that 'what has happened is a symptom of a much larger and more complicated problem', namely that 'the entire post-Cold War European political and security architecture was built on the foundation of two institutions – the European Union and NATO – which did not include Russia'.[12] The West, they note, gambled that Russia would accept these institutions, which proved to be a bad wager. Instead, more thought should have been given to a new post-Cold War regional order that Russia could have joined.

This argument is a worthy one to consider, and we explore it below. The decisions made between German reunification in 1989 and the decision to enlarge the EU and NATO in 1993 and 1994 led, largely inadvertently, to a regional order in Europe that could not feasibly incorporate Russia. Yet this shortcoming cannot fully account for the current conflict between Russia and the West. For quite a few years, Russia had an often unhappy but nonetheless functional relationship with the Euro-Atlantic institutions. It could have persisted if there had not been a test of wills in post-Soviet Eurasia. Clearly, the possibility that NATO and the EU might eventually assimilate, in some way, all of Russia's neighbours, but not Russia itself, was a worry for the Kremlin, and one determinant of its intemperate reaction to the Maidan Revolution. But the decision to extend those institutions' outreach into post-Soviet Eurasia was made over the course of a decade after the mid-1990s, as one element of a broader contest for influence in the region. It is this contest that grew into a negative-sum interaction, and this contest that will be the focus of our book.

While the lack of an inclusive post-Cold War architecture was a precondition for the Ukraine crisis, this ruinous outcome could have been averted without revisiting the fundamentals of the European order. It was the contestation over the lands between Russia and the West that led to the explosion in Ukraine and sent tensions spiralling out of control.

We begin the next chapter with an examination of the foundational years of the post-Cold War order (from the late 1980s to the mid-1990s), since decisions taken in that period foreclosed the opportunity to erase completely the continent's dividing lines. Had that opportunity been seized, it could have headed off the Ukraine crisis and the broader regional contestation that long antedates it. Our book elides those disputes between Russia and the West since 1991 that did not bear directly on this negative-sum game – such as divergences over Russia's wars in Chechnya, ballistic-missile defence, the US occupation of Iraq, the civil war in Syria and the Western military intervention in Libya, to name just a few. This is not just a matter of establishing a clear scope. All these episodes did, to varying degrees, harm relations between Russia and the West. But the damage was limited and manageable. By contrast, the tensions resulting from the regional contestation that culminated in the Ukraine crisis were neither limited nor manageable. An understanding of the origins of the crisis is thus central to explaining how we got to this low ebb in Russia–West ties and how we might get out of it.

A brief word about geographic references: Historians, politicians and opinion-makers argue endlessly about the appropriate descriptors for countries and regions on the world map. For the lands that populate this book, there are a host of disputed terms: Eastern Europe, East Central Europe, Central Europe, Russia and Eurasia are prominent among them. Settling these terminological debates is beyond our remit here. We will avoid the phrases Eastern Europe and Central Europe, although we will quote them verbatim if characters in our story utter them. We will use East Central Europe to refer to the states that were part of the Soviet-dominated Warsaw Pact during the Cold War and are now members of NATO and the EU, and thus of the West. Russia will be used to refer to the post-Soviet state that under its constitution bears the dual moniker Russia and the Russian Federation. Eurasia is the most loosely defined of these terms, describing a space that spans the continental divide between Europe and Asia. We will apply the label post-Soviet Eurasia to the area occupied by the successor states to the Soviet Union. For a few years after 1991, post-Soviet Eurasia may be said to have covered the three Baltic countries (Estonia, Latvia and Lithuania), but they speedily exited the category and will be treated in the bulk of what follows as part of East Central Europe.

CHAPTER ONE

Cold Peace

Where to find the roots of the disastrous scene at the Donetsk airport? One might well look to background factors such as Russian imperialism, ancestral enmities over language and religion, Soviet nationality practices, and the micro-history of Crimea and the Donbas. Although variables like these are germane at some level of abstraction, our emphasis is on dynamics in the relative foreground.

The Ukraine crisis, as we see it, comes out of self-reinforcing adversarial behaviour in the post-Soviet section of the Eurasian macroregion. Stretching over a quarter-century but gathering momentum in the second half of that time span, this contest has given rise to a belt of instability, insecurity and discontent of which Ukraine is but one part. The multidimensional rivalries percolating there encapsulate three 'geos' pursued by states and blocs of states: geopolitics, which is standard-issue realpolitik with special attention to attaining influence over particular countries or areas; geo-economics, or the projection of power over territory using economic means, an exercise defined by 'the logic of war in the grammar of commerce';[1] and geo-ideas, by which we mean policies to spread normative conceptions of the good and the right beyond national borders.[2]

The current chapter tells the tale of the Cold Peace, in Boris Yeltsin's evocative phrase. It is bookended by the implosion of the Soviet Union's zone of external hegemony at the end of the 1980s, which, despite the giddiness of the moment, left some bedrock issues unresolved, and a natural inflection point in 2003–04, the highlight of which was the 'colour revolutions' that tore through several post-Soviet states. Later chapters will deal with the more conflictual periods to come.

The settlement-that-wasn't

The Cold War between West and East, centred on if not confined to Europe, came undone with amazing swiftness. The outcome, while an undeniable advancement on the way things were, fell short of the promise of a continent united and democratically governed, as many had hoped. We are still living with the consequences of the unfinished business.

Europe had been cleaved for decades along geopolitical, geo-economic and geo-ideational lines. It hosted two bristling military alliances (NATO to defend Western Europe and North America, and the Warsaw Pact for the Soviet Union and its six-country bloc in East Central Europe); two economic unions (the European Community, or EC, and the Council for Mutual Economic Assistance, or COMECON); and two ideological camps (espousing liberal democracy in the west, and collectivist autocracy in the east). The Berlin Wall, replete with barbed wire, watchtowers and minefields, epitomised the continent's disunion.

Seismic changes originated with Mikhail Gorbachev, the general secretary appointed by the Soviet 'selectorate' in 1985. Gorbachevian *perestroika* was about 'new thinking' in foreign policy as well as remaking the Soviet Union's hidebound internal systems. He began a loosening of the ties that bound the USSR's European vassals – Poland, East Germany (also known as the German Democratic Republic, or GDR), Czechoslovakia, Hungary, Romania and Bulgaria – to Moscow, and nudged them to mount their own perestroikas. Gorbachev's acknowledgement in March 1988 that all socialist countries had 'the inalienable right to decide independently their developmental path' signified the repeal of the 'Brezhnev Doctrine' of using all means necessary, including armed intervention, to prevent defection from the bloc.

The Kremlin originally intended for change in its camp to be evolutionary; inadvertently, it opened the floodgates to revolutionary change. Marxist-Leninist governments fell one by one in a tumultuous six-month stretch in 1989, commencing with the electoral victory of the Solidarity labour movement in Poland in June and closing in December with the execution by firing squad of Romanian dictator Nicolae Ceauşescu. The Berlin Wall was sundered on 9 November and chunks of it carted off by jubilant spectators as souvenirs. In 1990 and 1991 came the reunification of Germany (and *ipso facto* the disappearance of the GDR), the self-liquidation of the Warsaw Pact and COMECON, and, most remarkable of all, the dismantlement of the Soviet Union and of the Soviet political-economic system. As the newly minted president of Czechoslovakia, the playwright and ex-dissident Václav Havel, was to tell the US Congress in February 1990, new developments were coming on at such a clip that 'none of the familiar political speedometers is adequate'.[3]

In Washington, the administration of George H.W. Bush, inaugurated in January 1989, shed its initial scepticism about changes in the area and set a goal 'to steer the Soviet ejection from Eastern Europe to a peaceful conclusion', as James Baker, his secretary of state, said candidly in a memoir.[4] For the Soviet

Politburo, coping with the vicissitudes of the bloc was but one of a plethora of challenges, not merely to policy objectives but to the governability and very survival of their state. At meetings with the Soviet foreign minister, Eduard Shevardnadze, Baker found him 'distracted and a little overwhelmed' by socio-economic woes and separatism on the home front and a feeling of 'losing control' across the board.[5]

The burning question on the security agenda in 1989–90 was what should be done with a post-Cold War Germany. Its frontline status in the Cold War, centrality to the two world wars, and sheer demographic and economic bulk made Germany distinctive. The Soviets were goaded to act by the death throes of their handiwork, the GDR. Leaders of the Federal Republic of Germany (aka West Germany) and the US stewed over the question of how long the opening for progress would last. Gorbachev could be dethroned, resign in exasperation or change his mind and order in the tanks, as the USSR had done against an East German workers' uprising in June 1953. 'We were running against a clock', Bush's national security adviser, Brent Scowcroft, wrote later, 'but we did not know how much time was left'.[6]

Gorbachev's initial goal was to administer German affairs through a revived Allied Control Commission of the occupying powers from 1945: the Soviet Union, the US, the UK and France. In 1989 he came out in favour of a bi-state Germany implanted in a 'common European home', a pan-European mansion of many diverse rooms, but with 'a certain integral whole'.[7] Gorbachev and his aides, notes Mary Sarotte, 'would never think their ideas through fully, and their plans would remain vague until the end'.[8] Chancellor Helmut Kohl of West Germany gravitated from a confederation of the two Germanys to the approach that was to prevail: outright reunification, and on Western terms.[9] Gorbachev signalled a green light for a merger in talks with Baker and Kohl in February 1990.[10] The details were thrashed out that summer and the deed was done in October (Kohl had first forecast the transition would take ten years). The GDR would be absorbed into the pre-existing structures of the Federal Republic, the consolidated Germany would stay put in the Euro-Atlantic alliance and the EC, force levels on all sides would be drawn down, no non-German NATO troops would be based on the territory of the former GDR and the 400,000 Soviet troops there would depart by 1994.

Gorbachev originally swore that he could never accept the reborn Germany as a member of NATO, the alliance dedicated to containing the USSR. He several times recommended Germany be incorporated into the Warsaw Pact, a non-starter, after which he was briefly enamoured of dual membership of NATO and the Pact. 'That made no sense to anyone on the American side', recollects Baker, 'but Gorbachev made a personal plea to the President [Bush]. "You're a sailor. You will understand that if one anchor is good, two anchors are better."' Bush scoffed at the concept to Kohl, calling it 'screwy'. Gorbachev's fallback was German neutrality, an outcome Soviet policy preferred back in the 1950s, but he was also willing to toy with fresh scenarios. With Baker in May 1990 he made the stunning suggestion that if he could not stop Germany from joining NATO, the Soviet Union itself should apply for membership. 'After all, you said that NATO wasn't directed against us, you said it was a new Europe, so why shouldn't we apply?' It was 'not some absurdity', he said, but a serious question. Baker rejoined that a journalist had put the same query to him at a news conference and was otherwise noncommittal, preferring to concentrate on Germany.[11]

Gorbachev was eventually won over to the American position that an amalgamated German state was more of a hazard to Soviet interests if non-aligned (and with the technical capabilities to go nuclear) than if knit into an alliance system. With the Warsaw Pact on the rocks, the sole alliance on offer was NATO. Gorbachev, Scowcroft writes, 'appeared unable to come up with a better idea than what we were urging on him'. Had he been resolute about German neutrality, 'he perhaps could have accomplished that'.[12]

The long-standing German problem was thus laid to rest. Two other daunting security questions were not: What would be the new regional order once the Warsaw Pact and COMECON had vanished? And how would its Soviet/Russian metropole relate to the Western camp?

On question number one, the USSR wagered on a body known as the Conference on Security and Co-operation in Europe (CSCE), to be renamed the Organization for Security and Co-operation in Europe (OSCE) in 1995. A child of the ephemeral East–West detente of the mid-1970s, it functioned as a roundtable for members of both alliances and Europe's neutral countries. At a CSCE summit in Paris in November 1990, 32 nations initialled a Charter of Paris for a New Europe, saluting as their target the 'Europe whole and free' first hailed by Bush in 1989.[13] Soviet delegates talked up the CSCE as a replacement for both the Warsaw Pact and NATO. But it was an informal grouping with a tiny staff and budget; it had no collective security mission or integrated military command; and it operated only by consensus. Unlike in NATO, which also has a consensus rule, there was no tradition of deferring to US preferences, which devalued the CSCE in the eyes of the Americans. The CSCE, as Baker summed it up, was 'an extremely unwieldy and frustrating organization' whose bylaws 'give the smaller states of Europe veto power over issues far beyond their standing'.[14]

In another tack, Gorbachev, in several pronouncements after he disowned the Brezhnev Doctrine, advocated the 'Finlandisation' of East Central Europe. Post-1945 Finland was neutral in foreign affairs, traded extensively with the Soviet Union and was self-governing in its domestic affairs. Gorbachev lauded Finlandisation during a visit to Helsinki in October 1989: 'To me, Finland is a model of relations between a big country and a small country, a model of relations between states with different social systems, a model of relations between neighbours.'[15] The former US secretary of state, Henry Kissinger, weighed in on Gorbachev's side. 'In the long run', he asked in an op-ed, 'aren't arrangements in Finland more useful to Soviet security than those in Eastern Europe? Is it possible to devise arrangements that would give the Soviets security guarantees (widely defined) while permitting the peoples of Eastern Europe to choose their own political future?'[16]

Neither recipe could have been implemented unrevised. For the CSCE to be the linchpin, it would have had to be boosted administratively and financially. At some point, it would have had to displace NATO and the EC as the primary regional organisation for collective security and economic integration. As long as the much heartier NATO and EC continued to function at their previous level and did not face challenges to their *raison d'être*, the West would have little incentive to empower an alternative body, particularly one where the heir to its long-time adversary had an equal say. Many regarded Finlandisation as tarnished by its power asymmetries, and Finnish–Soviet relations since 1945 had fluctuated over time; Finlandisation was not one prototype but several.[17] A more relevant precedent may have been 'Austrianisation', harkening back to the imposition of neutrality on post-war Austria by great-power dictate in 1955. It was missing from the conversation, other than a succinct reference by Kissinger in June 1990.[18]

The 22 NATO and Warsaw Pact states in November 1990 signed a Treaty on Conventional Armed Forces in Europe (CFE), delineating ceilings for armaments for what were still the two blocs, and created an inspection and verification regime to build confidence and reinforce stability. A follow-up at Helsinki in 1992 set limits on military personnel. Other than the CFE, which was about hardware and manpower and not about how or against whom they were to be used, no all-encompassing security framework for Europe was given serious consideration in the twilight of the Cold War. The Warsaw Pact, the 'socialist community' that it shielded having melted away, voted to disband in February 1991; COMECON followed suit that June. The Western duo of NATO and the EC was now the only game in town.

The talks over Germany not only yielded agreement on it remaining within NATO after reunification but also touched upon the future of the Alliance, and by implication of the security architecture of the extended region. This far-ranging issue was to be a future bone of contention. At a sitting with Gorbachev in February 1990, Baker enunciated the United States' willingness to pledge 'no extension of NATO's jurisdiction for forces of NATO [sic] one inch to the east' upon reunification. Baker was addressing the question of whether NATO forces would be barred from the territory of the GDR, as the Soviets were demanding. But this and other diplomatic exchanges left the Soviet negotiators with the distinct impression that the prohibition would transcend East Germany and cover the other five nations stranded in the Warsaw Pact (Bulgaria, Czechoslovakia, Hungary, Poland and Romania). The latter position, as Joshua Shifrinson has documented, was mooted in some inter-agency memos in Washington and had been spelled out by the West German foreign minister, Hans-Dietrich Genscher. Enlarging NATO beyond Germany was not on the table for anyone at the time; the Soviets, it has to be stressed, now believed that it would never be. The US and West Germany delivered informal assurances on limiting NATO's geographical reach, on respect for Soviet core interests and on cooperatively figuring out a comprehensive security framework, perchance through a revamped CSCE. As Baker put it in a memo after one confab with Shevardnadze, the process 'would not yield winners and losers. Instead, [it] would produce a new legitimate European structure – one that would be inclusive, not exclusive.'[19]

Gorbachev in particular bought into a broad reading of the spirit of the interchanges with the Americans, and it – plus, one has to think, a dose of wishful thinking – weighed heavily in his acceptance of the reunification scheme. When NATO several years later began preparations to take in new members to the east, he cried foul, as has each successive Russian leader since.[20] In Shifrinson's judgement, the Russians 'are essentially correct' in their grievance. 'NATO expansion was to violate ... the quid pro quo at the heart of the diplomacy that culminated in German reunification within NATO.'[21] The policymakers who subsequently chose to enlarge NATO, to be fair, did not think that such a quid pro quo ever existed. But this divergence in views itself indicates that the overarching issue was not truly resolved. In terms of the politics of it, this 'settlement-that-wasn't' became vulnerable to allegations *ex post facto* in Moscow, either that the West acted in bad faith, or that Gorbachev should have held out for better terms instead of giving away the store.

An aspect of the German reunification procedure that bears emphasis is the reliance on what Sarotte discerningly couches as 'prefab' change, a methodology hinged on the mechanical extension of existing formulas and structures rather than negotiation of mutually acceptable substitutes for them. Not only did the Federal Republic literally absorb the GDR into its pre-existing constitutional and legal order, but the newly reunified state was a full member of NATO and of the EC (to be elevated in 1993 into a European Union) to boot. Prefab had its virtues: it 'wasted no time on conceptualizing new accords and institutions', it did not set out to fix what was not broken, and it 'conferred a strong element of predictability on the chaotic … overhaul of both domestic and international order'.[22] In the case of German reunification, the prefab approach also paid off in almost everyone's estimation, so much so that it became a template. To join the winners' club, other countries must change themselves to conform with its existing rules; the institutions do not change in order to take on new members.

The paradox was, as Sarotte notes, 'the struggle to recast Europe after the momentous upheaval of 1989 resulted in prefabricated structures from before the upheaval moving eastward and securing a future for themselves. Americans and West Germans had successfully entrenched the institutions born of the old geopolitics of the Cold War world – ones that they already dominated, most notably NATO – in the new era.'[23] The counter-scenarios emanating sporadically out of Moscow – great-power condominium, a pan-European home, Finlandisation and so on – were half-baked and were discarded sequentially under the pressure of time and circumstance. Faced with a choice between a leap into the unknown and reliance on a proven model, Western policymakers' instinct was to shun vague, if high-minded, concepts and stick with the familiar.

Another thorny complication of the settlement-that-wasn't of 1989–91 bore on the soon-to-be-former Soviet superpower. Absent any act of reconciliation with the West, and any formal agreement to record and enforce it, no one could know where it fit in the new/old scheme of things. The quick fix of prefab did not delineate any definite place for it, not out of conscious malice but because it was too unwieldy to conform to the rigid standards. As a result, to borrow Sarotte's words, 'Russia was left on the periphery of a post-Cold War Europe'.[24] The country agent in her sentence is *Russia*, the Soviet Union having gone extinct at the end of the two years.

A flotilla of successor states, formerly constitutive 'union republics' of the USSR, which fell apart as the central government and the Communist Party lost their grip, set sail as 1991 came to a close. In their midst was Russia, formally co-titled the Russian Federation (identified until then as the RSFSR, the Russian Soviet Federative Socialist Republic), which became the agreed legal successor of the Soviet state, and took over its embassies, its veto-bearing seat in the UN Security Council and the lion's share of its awesome arsenal of weapons of mass destruction. This new Russia, its top offices housed in the same midtown Moscow buildings as their Soviet precursors, encompassed 77% of the USSR's landmass (16.4m square kilometres), 51% of its population (147.4m), 70% of its manufacturing and 91% of the oil pumped. That said, it was no Soviet Union. Territorial contraction and political and economic turmoil (its GDP dropped calamitously by 40% between 1991 and 1998) diminished it in almost every objective respect and in the subjective assessments of onlookers. While the Russian Federation was nominally a brand-new state, and not a rump USSR minus its non-Russian parts, its citizens and elite saw themselves as heirs to the Soviet legacy. Loath as the Americans and Germans were to say it out loud, the unwinding of two quasi-empires – an outer one in East Central Europe, an inner one in post-Soviet Eurasia – amounted to a staggering defeat for the 'Russian' state. Trauma stemming from this loss of face was inevitable and would need to be well managed – which it was not, to the detriment of all.

The proliferation of the *other* offspring of the Soviet Union was no less bewildering than the advent of a downsized Russia. A few had fought for their independence; the rest accepted it when it fell into their laps after the republic leaders of Belarus, Russia and Ukraine signed the December 1991 Belavezha Accords, which declared the end of the USSR. Nine of the 14 were sandwiched between the Russian Federation, East Central Europe and NATO member Turkey; the other five were in faraway Central Asia. Eleven of those 14 assented to join a loose-knit supranational Commonwealth of Independent States (CIS) along with Russia.[25] The three Baltic republics (Estonia, Latvia and Lithuania), having declared independence as early as August 1991, boycotted the CIS. It was a mark that they were already positioning themselves in the East Central European category, a move strongly backed by the US and not much resisted by Russia.[26]

The newcomers were internationally recognised and had seats in the UN and the CSCE (membership of which ballooned to 53). They would waste no time acquiring diplomatic services, border posts and national armies, and all the other trappings of statehood.[27]

The problem of the In-Betweens

On what principles was a post-Cold War order in the region to rest? After the dust of 1989–91 had settled, the answer was still unclear, although two of the suite advanced in the 1990 Charter of Paris for a New Europe offered clues. On the one hand, the document heralded national 'freedom of choice' on security matters. On the other, it nodded to a principle of 'indivisibility': 'Security is indivisible and the security of every participating State is inseparably linked to that of all the others.' The two tenets pointed in opposing directions, as time was to tell.

At the very start, the post-communist states of East Central Europe advanced incremental security remedies, such as reform of the Warsaw Pact and dialogue with NATO. More ambitiously, Czechoslovakia plugged a CSCE-based European Security Commission to supplant both venerable alliances. The outgoing Bush administration punted, getting NATO to birth a North Atlantic Cooperation Council whose parleys were good for 'a photo op and an exercise in high political symbolism' but little else.[28] It also urged the East Central Europeans to get hold of regional security measures on their own. Only in 1993, with the arrival of Bill Clinton in the White House, did Western policy planners engage in the process, with the Americans taking the lead.

They did so in part at the behest of the leaders of the erstwhile Soviet satellites who jettisoned their original reticence and pleaded for consideration of what up until then would have seemed an indecently radical response – admission of their nations to the NATO alliance. Motivations in East Central Europe were sundry, but the irreducible one was to find an international anchor – the same analogy Gorbachev employed with Bush in 1990 – in an environment awash in insecurity and unpredictability.

A majority of the players in the US government, including cabinet secretaries, diplomats, military brass and mid-level political appointees, preferred at the outset to leave the composition of NATO as it was, without recruitment of new members. Changes to NATO, it was argued, would subvert other priorities and be of no real benefit to it as a military organisation. More disconcerting was the chance that enlarging NATO would empower revanchist factions within the Russian polity and weaken Yeltsin. As Strobe Talbott, Clinton's lieutenant for Russian affairs, expressed it, 'If NATO adopted an anti-Russian rationale for taking in new members, it could tip the balance of forces in Russian politics in exactly the direction that we … most feared.'[29] The sceptics lost the debate to a handful of pro-change policy entrepreneurs, spearheaded by Anthony Lake, Clinton's national security adviser, and a bit later by Richard Holbrooke, then an assistant secretary of state.

The Russian response was scattershot. Not surprisingly, a sizeable subset of the Moscow establishment wanted nothing to do with an expanded NATO. The Foreign Intelligence Service spoke for them in late 1993 when it published a report warning that admission of former communist states 'will be taken by a considerable part of Russian society as "the approach of danger to the Motherland's borders"'.[30] Yeltsin took a middle position, maintaining that NATO's growth might be acceptable on one condition – that Russia be included in the process, as Gorbachev had hinted at for the Soviet Union several years before. He set this idea down in a letter to Clinton on 30 September 1993, and mentioned it in public on several occasions in 1994.[31] Meanwhile, Yeltsin's foreign minister, Andrei Kozyrev, argued that enlargement was unnecessary since all states concerned, Russia included, were learning how to cooperate with NATO, and vice versa. In a December 1993 interview, he seemed to be asking what the fuss was all about: 'We say to the [East Central Europeans]: why chomp at the bit to get into NATO when there is no need? Russia cooperates with the alliance, and you can do the same thing. But it's not worth it to enlarge NATO quantitatively.'[32]

It was in large part in deference to Russia that NATO's first initiative was a soft-edged Partnership for Peace (PfP) programme approved in December 1993, with eligibility for any member of the North Atlantic Cooperation Council interested in working with the Alliance. For a time, PfP seemed to push NATO enlargement off the agenda. The US secretary of state, Warren Christopher, had sold PfP to Yeltsin in October as a transitional device, egalitarian in philosophy and of indeterminate duration. 'There would be no effort to exclude anyone and there would be no step taken at this time to push anyone ahead of others.' Yeltsin, with the tenet of indivisibility at the back of his mind, was delighted with the project and got Christopher to agree that the affiliation 'would ... be on an equal footing and there would be a partnership and not a membership'. 'It would have been an issue for Russia', Yeltsin went on, if the PfP rulebook 'left us in a second-class status', but on these terms he was eager to have Russia put in an oar. Christopher added, 'we will in due course be looking at the question of membership [in NATO] as a longer term eventuality. ... Those who wish to can pursue the idea over time, but that will come later.'[33]

Not long thereafter, however, Clinton proclaimed in Prague that the question about enlargement was 'no longer whether ... but when and how'.[34] Within months, 'in due course' and 'longer-term eventuality' had flown out the window and the NATO capitals were horse-trading over the details. After a breather so as not to jinx Yeltsin's re-election chances in the 1996 presidential campaign, the admission process accelerated in late 1996 and invitations to the Czech Republic (having separated from Slovakia in 1993), Hungary and Poland were issued in 1997. They were received into the Alliance at a 50th-jubilee summit in April 1999.

Three considerations tilted the scales in American deliberations and shaped the United States' general stance toward this part of the world. One, rightly or wrongly, was a guilty conscience over having let down its inhabitants in the past. This sentiment was regularly embodied in historical analogies: to the Munich Agreement of 1938, to the Holocaust, and especially to the Yalta Conference of 1945, where the Big Three (Winston Churchill, Franklin D. Roosevelt and Joseph Stalin) decided the fate of post-war Europe over the heads of the countries affected. A second factor was ideological. Clinton, Lake and Holbrooke, as James Goldgeier writes, 'were intellectual heirs of Woodrow Wilson, believing that the expansion of international institutions and the promotion of freedom in economic and political affairs could increase global peace and prosperity'.[35] The international institutions worthy of this task were those led by or yoked to the US. The third consideration was elementary. A bigger footprint for the Alliance would lock in previous American gains, maximise American power and facilitate American do-gooding.

US policymakers, to quote Stephen Sestanovich, ambassador-at-large for the former Soviet Union in Clinton's second term, sought a new world order erected on shared values. 'But they also sought to preserve and strengthen America's place in the post-Cold War balance of power. The two goals seemed inseparable. Washington saw no other way to make its hopeful world order a reality. NATO enlargement was part and parcel of this reality.'[36] It exemplified, in other words, geopolitics married to geo-ideas. Justification was found in the principle of freedom of choice, one of the two keystones of the Charter of Paris. Individual countries, and they alone, should decide on what security alignments were to their liking. If any or all of the post-communist nations of East Central Europe threw in their lot with the US-shepherded Euro-Atlantic alliance, no other state – the United States included, ironically – could question that choice.

Not only were there benefits to be reaped, but the costs were largely seen as negligible. Popular interest in the enlargement issue, pro and con, was thin in the US and other NATO member states. 'Many opponents bemoaned the lack of visible public debate for such a major foreign policy initiative', writes Goldgeier. 'But why would the public be interested in what appeared to be a low-cost extension of a defense commitment in a benign strategic environment?'[37] Potential censure from Moscow, the only real obstacle, was deemed surmountable by American and European officials. They reckoned, correctly, that Russia was so enervated by its post-communist transformation that it could not block enlargement, and their Western-leaning counterparts like Kozyrev did not seem overly bothered by it.

Nor were the analytical costs prohibitive. No soul-searching or intellectual heavy lifting was required. German reunification offered a convenient template. Its prefab logic required aspirants to membership of the club to demonstrate a zeal for admission and proof of their credentials under a pre-existing formula. Prefab change by definition did not allow for adjustment of the formula or give-and-take among current and prospective members about its design, thus excluding countries (like Russia) that demanded a say in such matters.

There were no genuine negotiations with Russia on the central issue of the merits of NATO's extension, let alone the details of the process. Attitudinal openness in Moscow gradually dissipated as awareness dawned that a joint search for a solution was not on the cards. Yeltsin grounded his early receptivity to talking about Russia-in-NATO in indivisibility, the second of the pillars of the Charter of Paris. Russia was comfortable inside a revised security framework only so long as its prerogatives and stature were taken into account, with all that connoted for the US having to share control. Change without Moscow's participation and consent was doomed to be interpreted as 'a sign that we were not welcome', as several former ranking Russian functionaries put it in interviews.

Clinton was agreeable to the theoretical possibility of Russian admission. In his administration, however, it was scripture that entry for Russia could be concretely entertained only after other countries had been dealt with. As Ronald Asmus, who ran enlargement policy in the Department of State in 1997–2000, testified later:

> Clinton had indulged Yeltsin on [the point of eligibility], while making it clear that this was not a realistic prospect any time soon. Internally, I often told my staff that we had the 10, 25, and 50-year plans. The

first was for Central and Eastern Europe, the second
for Ukraine, and the third for Russia.

Christopher's 'no one ahead of others' had morphed into
'everyone ahead of Russia'. By now even whispers of a hypothetical Russian membership bid fuelled antagonism. Asmus
reports American trepidation that Moscow 'might try ... to
create mischief by actually applying for membership'. When
Kozyrev's hard-nosed successor as foreign minister, Yevgeny
Primakov, mooted an application in 1996, the response from
Talbott was terse: 'Russia would have to get into the same queue
and meet the same criteria as other candidates.' Primakov
suspected the Americans of trying to trick the Russians into
a premature statement of intent, which could then be used to
refute any objections to other applications.[38]

At work under the surface was the bare-knuckled calculus of security. NATO spokespersons trumpeted that their
policy was not anti-Russian. That may have been true, but the
leaders of the aspirants to membership seldom concealed the
fact that they considered it more than anything else a hedge
against revanchism by Russia, a point echoed by a number of
Western strategists. Even if the policy was not expressly anti-
Russian, Russia was for all practical purposes disqualified from
partaking and had no guarantees whatsoever against future
encroachment on its interests. Where the diplomacy of the late
1980s had rested on an amorphous dream of assimilation into
Western and global systems, 'the 1990s were marked by the
steady atrophy of serious efforts to integrate Russia'.[39]

Yeltsin and his government for some time continued their
late Soviet predecessors' touting of the CSCE/OSCE as an alternative to a widened NATO. In May 1994 they proposed to
outfit it with 'a leadership organ of restricted composition', a
compact executive board modelled on the UN Security Council

whose members – one of them Russia – would have veto rights. This was in a sense the Russian edition of prefab institutional design, applying an antecedent model to current problems. But no sympathy for its version of OSCE reform was forthcoming from the West, from aspirants to NATO or from the smaller countries that felt they would lose from a potent executive.[40]

The best Moscow could manage by way of damage limitation and a consolation prize was the Founding Act on Mutual Relations, Cooperation and Security between NATO and the Russian Federation, an agreement signed in Paris in May 1997. As Primakov stated in his memoirs, the Russian aim was 'not to drop our negative position on NATO expansion' and at the same time to work out ways to 'minimise the consequences that were most threatening to our security and most inconsistent with our interests'. In conversations in the wings, Primakov warned that admission of any ex-Soviet republic hereafter was 'unacceptable' and would traverse a 'red line' for Russia.[41] The Founding Act stated that NATO and Russia 'do not consider each other as adversaries' and 'share the goal of overcoming the vestiges of earlier confrontation and competition and of strengthening mutual trust and cooperation'.[42]

Any goodwill emanating from the Founding Act was dispelled by a bitter controversy over the 1999 NATO air war against Slobodan Milosevic's Yugoslav government, which had forcibly repressed a revolt by the Kosovar Albanian minority. It was the first major intervention in the history of the Alliance and the first to implement revisions of NATO's strategic concept that allowed for military actions other than territorial defence. Incensed over the bombing campaign, Moscow broke off liaison with NATO and made the risky decision to send airborne troops into Pristina, Kosovo, ahead of the allied forces. Although cooler heads eventually prevailed and Russia contributed to the NATO-led peacekeeping mission in Kosovo, official suspicion hit new heights and Russian popular opinion was agitated. The episode underscored the growing gap between Russia and NATO over the Alliance's post-Cold War modus operandi, particularly its enlargement and 'out-of-area' actions like Kosovo. Talk of Russia's potential membership had almost ceased.

A parallel geo-economic dynamic took shape in the form of the European Union's growth ambitions and the beginning of its enlargement process to take in the East Central European countries in the mid-1990s. EU enlargement followed its own prefab logic: the main qualification for membership was whole-sale adoption of the *acquis communautaire*, the EU's manual of laws and regulations. Russia signed a much less ambitious Partnership and Cooperation Agreement (PCA) with the EU in June 1994, and took a mostly benign attitude toward the Union. Individual member states and not the EU bureaucracy in Brussels called the shots in the relationship at this time. The EU member-state governments were mostly interested in commercial diplomacy, notably Germany with its booming export-oriented industries. Moscow and Brussels agreed a Four Common Spaces programme in 2005 as a framework to substitute for the EU–Russia PCA after its expected expiration in 2007, and conducted biannual summits.

But trouble was brewing in the background. The EU based its enlargement process on 'insistence on the universal appli-cability of its internal mode of governance [i.e., the *acquis*]', claiming what has been termed 'normative hegemony' over its neighbourhood. The pretence was to something like a geo-ideational unipolar moment on the continent. Brussels evinced a patronising attitude in its dealings with proximate coun-tries: it did not give them 'any meaningful input in setting the normative agenda … it is only willing to give its neighbors a say on *when* they will implement its demands, not *how*', as the

Finnish scholar Hiski Haukkala puts it.[43] This was all well and good for the East Central Europeans, who were willing to do whatever was asked of them to get into the club. But Moscow would not adopt such prefab Western solutions without any say in their content.

Even if Russia had sought membership of NATO or the EU, the organisations would not have been able to absorb such a large country with the multiplicity of economic, social and security problems that would have come with it – unless they were to change dramatically to accommodate that challenge. But the basic premise of the prefab approach was that the rules were not negotiable. The institutions do not change to accommodate aspirants; the aspirants change themselves in order to become members. Russian officials, who still saw their country as a great power, never had this 'normal' membership process in mind when they broached the idea. As Sestanovich writes, 'Russian officials would have had to endure insufferable Western bossiness, high-handed and irritating Western lectures, and insulting Western reviews of whether Russia was abiding by its "Membership Action Plan". NATO didn't want to start down that road any more than the Russians did.'[44] The same could have been said about the EU. The Russians wanted to be at the table as equals, and were mystified as to why the West would not waive the usual requirements for the sake of partnership.

The psychological fallout from the heir to a superpower being denied an authentic voice in shaping the regional order and told to wait its turn to get in – Gulliver standing in line behind the Lilliputians — was evident to sophisticated observers.[45] Its significance was grievously underestimated by those in positions to do something about it.

Western and Russian policies come across in retrospect as unimaginative and incommensurate with the magnitude of the possibilities unlocked by the termination of the Cold War, and thereby as complicit in sowing the anger and mistrust that soon took hold. It was in a speech at Budapest in December 1994, as the direction things were taking was becoming clear, that Yeltsin famously dubbed the new normal the Cold Peace – not warlike, but not friendly or deeply collaborative either.

The West fancied the comfort of prefab change over original design. The prioritisation of NATO and EU enlargement relegated the OSCE to the backwaters of European security and integration efforts. Dangling the possibility of Russia partaking in its alliance system, the West consigned the practicalities to some Neverland, long after present company were dead. It drew the false lesson from Moscow's inability to stop the enlargement process that future Russian complaints could also be dismissed without consequence.[46] As for Russia, time and again it seemed to sink more effort into critiquing Western schemes than into fleshing out its own. It broached a CIS–NATO alliance without setting the idea to paper or discussing it with its CIS associates. It flirted with asking for NATO membership (as Gorbachev had done), yet never got around to doing so or to voicing an opinion on what would need to change to make it feasible.

Working away all along were the self-interested country scripts that realist theories of international relations would predict. For the countries of East Central Europe, once emancipated by the Soviet collapse, affiliations with the Western clubs were unsurpassed aids for balancing against the time-honoured Soviet/Russian hegemon. The overnight dissolution of the Soviet bloc and of the USSR itself licensed them to migrate from balancing to bandwagoning with the triumphant Western alliance, and then to jump from the bandwagon right into playing trombone in the band.

But another script was also unfolding. Although there has been some backsliding in recent years, on the whole NATO and particularly EU enlargement undergirded the development of secure and pluralistic market democracies. The prefab model empowered both organisations to reshape institutions of governance and impose Western rules on countries eager to 'rejoin Europe', as the saying went. The success of the transition from communism was no foregone conclusion in the early 1990s. As the Arab Spring has recently demonstrated, shifts from authoritarianism on this scale are often violent and inconclusive. The prefab model was a quintessential factor in the transformation of a wide swath of post-communist Europe.[47]

The lack of an inclusive regional order did not prevent many non-trivial acts of cooperation and benevolence across the old East–West fault line after 1991. But the foreign-policy realm Russia scrutinised most diligently was its neighbourhood, where the political map had been profoundly reshaped since Gorbachev opened Pandora's box. Given the fait accompli of an ever-larger NATO and, with a slight lag, an ever-larger EU, the countries of East Central Europe, including the Baltic trio, were fully absorbed into Western systems. Even hardliners in Moscow recognised that they were gone for good.

In another category entirely were the quintet of ex-Soviet republics in Central Asia. Landlocked and secluded from the European theatre, they were in no danger of decamping to the West; in fact, China soon became a much more palpable force there than Western governments or institutions. Two of them (Kazakhstan and Turkmenistan) owned shoreline on the Caspian Sea but did not share a land border with a member or prospective member of NATO or the EU. The Central Asians have thus played a secondary role in our story. Their importance as a great-power playground temporarily grew during the US-led operation in Afghanistan following 9/11 but faded following the exit of most combat troops in 2014.[48]

The critical area of interest for our story consists of six 'In-Betweens', that is, former Soviet republics flanked by Russia and East Central Europe. Belarus, Ukraine and Moldova were situated to Russia's west and southwest; Georgia, Armenia and Azerbaijan constituted the South Caucasus, a mountainous area lying between the Black and the Caspian seas. Belarus, Ukraine, Georgia and Azerbaijan bordered Russia; Moldova and Armenia were separated from it by a few hundred kilometres. Their combined 962,762 sq km was 6% of Russia's land area, but their population, 82.1m, was 56% of that of the erstwhile imperial metropole. They varied on characteristic after characteristic: cartographic location, climate, size, economic conditions, language, religious tradition, past association with Russia. Still, they shared much history, remote and recent, Russian as a lingua franca, a multitude of informal practices and norms, and a visceral reaction to – and propensity to manoeuvre around – any foreign policy made in Moscow.

Ukraine, the state with which Russia's relations were to be the rockiest, held custody of 63% of the In-Betweens' population (51.8m) and 58% of their landmass (579,330 sq km). Russia had a latent territorial grievance against Ukraine over the Crimean peninsula, which had been reassigned from RSFSR to Ukrainian jurisdiction by Nikita Khrushchev and the Soviet leadership in 1954. Acrimony flared up over proprietorship of the Soviet Black Sea Fleet, headquartered in Sevastopol, Crimea, which had 100,000 personnel and 835 ships in 1991. A treaty of 'friendship, cooperation and partnership' sealed by Yeltsin and the Ukrainian president Leonid Kuchma in May 1997 set aside the territorial issue. Separate agreements partitioned the fleet, with Moscow buying out much of the Ukrainians' share in exchange for debt relief, and provided Russia a 20-year lease on the naval base in Sevastopol and the right to billet 25,000 sailors, aviators and marines there.

Taken together, Russia, the Central Asians and the In-Betweens formed a unique post-imperial landscape. Unlike the lost overseas empires of Britain and France or the exploded empires of the Ottomans and Habsburgs, in this case the former empire is arrayed around the ex-metropole physically. Russia's central location gives it immense advantages in dealing with its neighbours. Centrality also begets a sense of vulnerability. A regime change in Pakistan or a shift in Australian foreign policy would have limited direct consequences for the UK. The same cannot be said about Georgia or Kazakhstan from the Kremlin vantage point, gazing out from the Moscow hub to spokes and rim. It can be no mystery why Russia, from Yeltsin onwards, has assiduously identified itself as having 'vital interests' in its post-Soviet Eurasian environs.

Using the standard measurements, the prerequisites of national power in post-Soviet Eurasia are more asymmetrically distributed than in any comparable global region other than the Americas.[49] Consider the raw facts about population magnitude and economic strength. In 2015, the ratio of Russia's population to that of its neighbours ranged from about three to one (for Ukraine) to more than 50 to one (for Armenia). In 2013 economic output, the range is much greater, from a ratio of ten to one (for Kazakhstan) to countries producing a fraction of 1% of Russia's output (Kyrgyzstan, Moldova and Tajikistan).

The legacy of Soviet planning augmented Russia's latent centripetal power. Gosplan (the economic-planning agency) had strewn production assets about Soviet territory with no regard for republic borders; without some degree of reintegration, or major alternative sources of growth, individual states would be stuck with a surfeit of inefficiencies. In a prescient paper written in the late 1990s, David A. Lake argued that it would be a mistake to assume that the demise of the USSR would be followed by an age of equality and disconnectedness between the neo-states:

The high level of relationally specific assets between the successor states, which remain as a residue of the old empire, will create important and voluntary pressures to rebuild some degree of economic and political hierarchy in the region. … Relations in the region will not look like those between autonomous, sovereign, 'Westphalian' states that characterize much of international politics. Rather, we are likely to find a range of relations, varying from protectorates to informal empires to empires and confederations.[50]

Given the power asymmetries, there would be only one candidate for originator and coordinator of a programme of partial reintegration – Russia.

As with the relationship *in toto*, it would stretch the truth to say that Russian–Western cooperation in post-Soviet Eurasia was non-existent in the 1990s. The outstanding case was the conjoint effort to counteract the dispersal of weapons from the USSR's nuclear storehouse. When the hammer-and-sickle was run down the Kremlin flagpole on 25 December 1991, 3,200 strategic warheads were located in Belarus, Kazakhstan and Ukraine, in storage or on intercontinental ballistic missiles and bomber aircraft, as were 4,000 of the less destructive tactical or non-strategic nuclear weapons. All of the tactical weapons were transported without incident to Russia by 1992. The Lisbon Protocol, brokered and co-signed by the Western powers the same year, bound Belarus, Kazakhstan and Ukraine to send their strategic warheads to Russia as well, where the fissile materials were to be converted into fuel for civilian reactors. There were no hiccups with Belarus and Kazakhstan; Ukraine resisted handing over its arsenal of 2,250 warheads, the third largest after Russia and the US. American pressure and aid were central to incentivising Ukraine to denuclearise.

In November 1994 Ukraine relented and joined the Nuclear Non-Proliferation Treaty as a non-nuclear-weapons state. The next month, Russia (with the US and Britain) gave its assent to a Budapest Memorandum solemnly obligating it 'to refrain from the threat or use of force against the territorial integrity or political independence of Ukraine'. The last nuclear weapons were shipped to depots in Russia in May 1996. Under the Cooperative Threat Reduction programme put forth by senators Sam Nunn and Richard Lugar, the American taxpayer footed much of the bill for deactivating the weapons, reprocessing the fissile material into reactor fuel and purchasing it for US power plants.[51]

Low-grade competition

Yet what typified the Cold Peace was not cooperation but the chilly disinterest insinuated by the catchphrase and the rise of competition in and over the In-Betweens, and to a lesser degree Central Asia. The competition was low-grade and muffled by situational factors, but competition all the same.

A starting point was the new Russia's avowal of geopolitical supremacy in post-Soviet Eurasia. Contrary to myth, this sense of entitlement was not the invention of Vladimir Putin after 1999. His more forward-thinking predecessor, Boris Yeltsin, laid it out unapologetically in a presidential decree on 'The Strategic Course of the Russian Federation with Respect to the Member States of the Commonwealth of Independent States', dated 14 September 1995. The decree is in force to the present day. 'On the territory of the CIS', it was affirmed, 'are concentrated Russia's most vital interests in the domains of economics, defence, security, and defence of [its citizens'] rights'. Russia was envisaged as a 'leading force in forming a new system of international … relations in the post-USSR space', and integral to this effort as acting 'to foster integrative processes in the CIS'.

In a sharply worded section on security, Yeltsin stipulated that Russian policy 'obtain from the CIS states performance of their obligations to desist from alliances and blocs directed against any of these states'. NATO should stay at arm's length, and the CIS countries should be in unison with Russia in waving a 'No Trespassing!' sign at interlopers. The decree allowed for cooperation with international organisations like the UN and the OSCE in regulating intra-regional conflicts, but underscored the need 'to get them to understand that *this region is first of all Russia's zone of influence*'.[52] The text on the face of it was a classic example of zero-sum geopolitics.

Russian attitudes towards the former Soviet republics were in flux in the 1990s. It was a decade of rampant uncertainty for all these countries, both domestically and in terms of their foreign relations. For the greenhorn Russian elite, many of whom had been in the Soviet, 'all-union', institutions just a few years earlier, acceptance of the other progeny of the USSR as fully sovereign countries did not come easily. For example, Vladimir Lukin, Moscow's ambassador to Washington, blithely told Talbott in 1993 that relations between Russia and Ukraine were to be 'identical to those between New York and New Jersey'.[53] Lukin was something of a liberal on the Russian political spectrum; Russian nationalists, who were well represented in parliament, were more menacing. One lawmaker warned in October 1992 against 'absolutising' the new borders dividing the former republics, since they were 'artificial' and 'arbitrary'.[54] Even Yeltsin, when he needed to protect his right flank, would indulge; for example, in March 1993 he called for 'international organisations' to grant Russia 'special authority as guarantor of peace and stability on the territory of the former USSR'.[55] The statement was not backed up by action, but it did inflame sensibilities across the region, eliciting angry retorts from several of the neighbours.

To have its way in post-Soviet Eurasia, the Russian Federation relied on a range of tools. It meddled persistently, though without a master plan, in the internal politics of the successor states, providing moral and media support, and from time to time funding, for groups receptive to Russian policy. In Ukraine, Russia threw its weight behind Yuri Meshkov, the head of the Crimean provincial government, who was a proponent of holding a referendum on secession of the peninsula from the rest of the country. When the national parliament dismissed him in 1995, he was granted asylum in Moscow. In most of the In-Betweens, Moscow's agencies maintained relations with representatives of diaspora Russian communities. Even moderates like Kozyrev spoke out for defence of the rights of Russians and Russian speakers in the former republics and their 'voluntary reintegration' with the Russian Federation.[56] A nationalist faction around Yuri Luzhkov, mayor of Moscow, were for a more venturesome policy and took a special interest in Crimea.

Russia kept military forces stationed in all of the In-Betweens and, for some time, in the Central Asian republics. Some of these garrisons resulted from its role as pacifier and mediator in the range of ethnic and political conflicts that broke out as the Soviet Union splintered. In Moldova, wedged between Ukraine and Romania, the Soviet and then Russian 14th Army defended the breakaway Transnistria in its conflict with Chisinau in 1990–92. Although unrecognised by any member of the United Nations, Transnistria has had self-rule ever since, and Russian peacekeepers and remnants of the 14th Army are still in place. In Georgia, Moscow brokered an end to two ethno-national wars between the Georgians and the South Ossetians (1991–92) and Abkhaz (1992–94), groups that had eponymous semi-autonomous provinces within the Georgian republic of the USSR. In Abkhazia, Russia's 'policy of divide and rule included military support to both sides in the conflict, which, over the course of the conflict, increasingly favored the [Abkhaz]', ministering to them with weapons, training and the odd airstrike on their Georgian adversaries.[57] The ceasefire agreements created Russian-dominated peacekeeping forces in both areas, along with diminutive international observer missions. Russia kept its army out of Nagorno-Karabakh, the breakaway province of Azerbaijan populated by ethnic Armenians that was the locus of a six-year-long succession of clashes, but it at one and the same time brokered a 1994 armistice in the fighting there, manned its Gyumri base in Armenia (thus warding off intervention by the Turks, ethnic cousins of the Azeris), promised to safeguard Yerevan's security and happily peddled arms all around. Moscow also intervened to put an end to the civil war of 1992–97 in Tajikistan, which had left more than 50,000 people dead.

In the early 1990s, Moscow's involvement in these crises was necessary (no other power was prepared to step in) and productive, in that it put a stop to bloodshed. Despite some misgivings in Washington, the US was generally empathetic; Clinton said in Moscow in January 1994, 'I think there will be times when you will be involved … in some of these areas near you, just like the United States has been involved in the last several years in Panama and Grenada near our area.'[58] The problems emerged after the guns had been silenced. With the exception of Tajikistan, all of the post-conflict arrangements Moscow brokered became mired in stalemate, earning these conflicts the 'frozen' label. The lack of political settlements provided a convenient rationalisation for maintaining Russian troops as peacekeepers in Abkhazia, South Ossetia and Transnistria, along with the bases in Armenia and Tajikistan, which the host governments welcomed. And Moscow had direct dealings with both recognised national governments and the separatist enclaves themselves. In Transnistria, South Ossetia and Abkhazia, Russia even began issuing passports to locals. Russian officials were often seconded, so to speak, to the separatist governments.

Economic instruments filled out the Russian toolbox. They were most often used to twist arms on particulars and to produce prosaic commercial advantage for Russian companies, but at times they did rise to the level of geo-economics. Centrality, purchasing power, resource endowment and the hardwired legacy of the Soviet economy gave Moscow substantial advantages. Even though Russia's economy was in contraction until the late 1990s, there was enough capital accumulation to facilitate investment abroad, including in disputed territories like Transnistria, South Ossetia and Abkhazia.[59] Energy afforded a special abundance of opportunities. Russia was the primary purveyor of oil and natural gas to all but the four other former Soviet republics that had their own hydrocarbon resources (Azerbaijan, Kazakhstan, Turkmenistan and, to a lesser extent, Uzbekistan); it routinely sold on credit and at below-market prices, making for buyer dependence. It also initially controlled all of the former USSR's export pipelines, including those leading to the profitable European gas market, giving it a financial lever with its four fellow exporters. At one time or another, it bullied uncooperative partners by raising energy prices or suspending deliveries, calling in debts, slapping tariffs on imports or excise taxes on exports, and restricting access for non-Russian oil and gas exporters to its pipelines. The scholar Daniel Drezner recorded 39 occasions when the Kremlin had recourse to such tactics between 1992 and 1997. It produced concessions in 15 cases, or 38%, a respectable rate of success by the standards of political economists.[60] Even success came at a price. By resorting to ham-fisted tactics whenever one of its neighbours did not behave to its liking, Russia aroused threat perceptions throughout the region and came to be more feared than trusted by local elites. The bullying also convinced hawks in Washington and European capitals that, if not reinforced, the independence of the post-Soviet states could be a passing phenomenon.

Russia did not limit itself to bilateral knobs and switches. It also operated through a bevy of multilateral institutions, of which the paramount in theory was the umbrella CIS. In the five years after its establishment in December 1991, the CIS stood up an executive secretariat in Minsk, an inter-parliamentary assembly and 12 coordinating councils (for heads of state, heads of government and ministers). It also spawned a flock of around 50 specialised bodies, dedicated to everything from patents to meteorology, civil aviation and plant breeding. All told, the CIS Council of Heads of State had adopted 500 documents by 2004, and the Council of Heads of Government more than 900; the vast majority of these agreements 'involved a relatively formal bureaucratic framework'.[61] Russian efforts were also devoted to more focused schemes for coordination of trade and development that smacked of geo-economics. In September 1993, a convocation of CIS heads of state adopted an Economic Union Treaty, featuring plans for a free-trade zone, a payments union and a monetary union. Subsidiary agreements on trade and tariffs, payments, legal harmonisation and rail transport ensued in 1994, 1995 and 1996. Steering power in the union was to be in proportion to economic output, so that Russia was in the driver's seat.

Russia inspired virtually all of the agreements inked. But cold realities belied ringing declarations of intent and the facade of teamwork. Not a few of the centrifugal forces unleashed by the disintegration of the USSR raged on unabated, making lofty goals, reports and guidelines all but unfulfillable. The parliament of Ukraine, a co-author of and the second-ranking member of the CIS, refused to ratify its charter. Ukrainian presidents dutifully attended CIS summit meetings while doing their best to 'derail Russian ideas as early on as at the level of experts, ministers, and prime ministers'.[62] In the ambit of economic coordination, the provisions of the 1993 treaty were honoured in the breach. Protectionism, national currencies (following the collapse of the short-lived rouble zone in 1993) and cumbersome banking rules were put in its place and intraregional trade plummeted by two-thirds. The centrality of the CIS accord was undercut by the decision of Russia, Belarus and Kazakhstan in 1995 to forge a trilateral customs union, which later garnered two more Central Asian adherents and the lofty title of the Eurasian Economic Community.[63] This entity, too, made little headway. Yet another geo-economic structure, the Single Economic Space (SES) among Russia, Belarus, Kazakhstan and Ukraine, was announced in September 2003.[64] In keeping with the trend, it proved to be another paper tiger.

Entropy was, if anything, more manifest in the security sphere. Six CIS members – Armenia, Kazakhstan, Kyrgyzstan, Russia, Tajikistan and Uzbekistan – had signed onto the Tashkent Treaty on collective security in 1992; three others (Azerbaijan, Belarus and Georgia) did so in 1993 and the treaty came into force in 1994. Lacking a common external enemy, the treaty had no practical consequences in the 1990s, particularly since several of its members were for all intents and purposes at war with each other. An institutional arm to carry out its provisions did not exist until the Collective Security Treaty Organization (CSTO) was created in 2002, ten years after the pact. Membership by that point was down to six: Russia, two of six In-Betweens (Armenia and Belarus) and three of five Central Asians (Kazakhstan, Kyrgyzstan and Tajikistan).[65] The CSTO operates out of a Moscow headquarters and conducts exercises among its members; in theory it has even had a rapid-reaction force at its disposal since 2009. In practice, the 'collective' element of its mission has, given power asymmetries, always been lacking; it functions mostly as a Russian security blanket for the smaller neighbours.

A close study of both security-and economic-policy fields by the Carnegie Endowment for International Peace found in 1999 that 'all of the post-Soviet states, including Russia, are too weak, distracted, and poor to be able to integrate'. 'Even the few common undertakings to which the CIS states have been able to agree have either been carried out shoddily or not at all, because neither Russia nor the other CIS states have the money to pay for them.'[66]

Nor did Russia have the organisational arena to itself. In October 1997 four In-Between abstainers or dropouts from the CSTO and the Economic Union Treaty formed a rival group known as GUAM, after the founding parties of Georgia, Ukraine, Azerbaijan and Moldova. GUAM was a talk shop about how to keep the Russians at bay and open up channels to the West (doing the talking in Russian, its official language). It gained observer status at the UN General Assembly in 2003, but would wait until 2006 to organise a secretariat (with all of eight staffers) in Kyiv. The member governments announced a free-trade area in July 2002 and signed a sprinkling of joint statements, installed a parliamentary assembly and working groups, and discussed at length a Europe–Caucasus–Asia Transport Corridor and a GUAM peacekeeping brigade. Little of substance came of these initiatives, which can be attributed to the same constellation of factors that plagued the Russia-led projects.[67] GUAM tried but was ultimately unable to widen its membership: Uzbekistan, which signed on in 2001 (making it GUUAM), ceased to participate in 2002 and abandoned it in 2005.

In the first decade or so after the Soviet collapse, the role of Western governments in these meanderings was modest.

The 1999 Carnegie Endowment study concluded that no CIS member state was a serious candidate for NATO admission, and that PfP was mostly of 'no more than a marginal influence', attuned to bland endeavours like search-and-rescue training rather than hard geopolitics.[68] The EU approach to post-Soviet Eurasia until 2004 was 'Russia first', other than allowing the three Baltics to apply for accession. As with NATO's efforts, the In-Betweens were involved only tangentially. Between 1995 and 1999, all six went for PCAs that provided for political dialogue and economic advice. Words almost universally outpaced deeds. Moldova may serve as an illustration: it 'repeatedly heralded European integration but did little to honor its obligations, and Europe remained only marginally interested in the small country'.[69]

American diplomats who served at the time recount that Washington's prime aim was to craft a 'presence' in every capital – an embassy, a military attaché, trade and aid missions, and so on – and to forge working relationships with the fledgling countries. Russian diplomats will say the Americans and less so the Europeans bad-mouthed all Russian integrationist moves as neo-Soviet. As one of them put it in an interview, 'They were constantly throwing a spanner in the works. ... Any action we took was considered an attempt to bring back the Soviet Union.'[70]

There is some truth to the Russian allegation. Inspired by Zbigniew Brzezinski, a former US national security adviser who warned in 1994 of Russia's 'proto-imperial' leanings, some policymakers did see Russia as bent on re-establishing an anti-Western bloc with the In-Betweens and the Central Asians.[71] The ritualistic endorsements of these states' sovereignty and territorial integrity intimated that Russia represented a threat to both. As then-US secretary of state Christopher brusquely put it, 'Russia must avoid any attempt to reconstitute the U.S.S.R.'[72] But the push to show the flag and the finger-pointing at an alleged Soviet-style approach to the region did not beget a Western eagerness to get tangled in local conflicts or to act systematically to thwart Russian policy. As one former practitioner recalls, 'Despite loud warnings from political and academic critics that Moscow was seeking to restore … control, many Western European states, and even the United States, accepted and at times welcomed Russian actions to stop the fighting and try to manage the conflicts on its periphery.'[73] In the early and mid-1990s, crises in the Persian Gulf and strife-torn Somalia and the Balkans seemed more salient, and absorption of the one-time Warsaw Pact states and the three Baltic countries was mission enough for even the most evangelical NATO supporters.[74] Primakov took pride in Russia's having made a place for OSCE and UN observers in its peacekeeping missions in Georgia, and remarked wryly that 'no one was in any hurry to replace the Russians, let alone to repeat what NATO had done in Bosnia'.[75]

Russia's economic woes spurred its neighbours to diversify their trade ties. The total exports of the 11 non-Russian CIS countries to the EU overtook the volume of their exports to Russia by 1998. The most prominent Western geo-economic incursion was occasioned by the bounteous petroleum reserves of the Caspian Sea basin. Oil- and gas-rich Azerbaijan, on the western coast, and Kazakhstan on the eastern, began to clamour for the liberty to deal with multinational oil companies without hindrance from Moscow even before December 1991. Multi-cornered wrangling in subsequent years produced a cavalcade of deals and joint ventures, many of them dead letters. The pinch point was transportation: getting the fuel to outside markets. Russia strived to monopolise this function through its pipeline network. Shevardnadze, now the Georgian president, and his counterpart Heydar Aliev of Azerbaijan lobbied for a route originating in Azerbaijan and stretching through Georgia to Ceyhan, a Turkish marine terminal on the Mediterranean. It was their brainchild that was eventually built, much to Russia's chagrin. A bureaucratic faction in Washington brought the US into the loop, on the grounds that 'it was incumbent upon the American government to come to the aid of the Caspian republics – in effect, to run interference for them against Russia'.[76] The geopolitical and geo-economic logic was that by breaking Russia's export monopoly, the new pipeline would provide both producer and transit countries with independent revenue streams, thus limiting Russian influence over their affairs. But the Clinton administration was also accommodating toward a second pipeline through Russia, and Moscow was restrained in its reaction to the setback. Russia had other fish to fry, the Caspian was a low priority for Yeltsin, and he was averse to the use of force to have his way, despite Shevardnadze's taking fright that the Russian military would 'blow me up' if he persisted.[77] Russia stayed out of the consortium but was free to lay down more pipe itself, which it did in later years. Agreement in principle on the 1,768km Baku–Tbilisi–Ceyhan Pipeline was reached in November 1998, ground was broken in 2003 and the first crude was pumped in 2005.

Stresses and strains

A frontal altercation over the allegiance of the In-Betweens did not materialise at this juncture. But this did not mean that all was sweetness and light. Stresses and strains grew in both significance and frequency in the late 1990s.

Unlike the East Central Europeans, the In-Betweens had diverse partialities and taller hurdles to clear – greater exposure to Moscow's hard and soft power, no historical memory of being part of Europe or national mission to 'return' to it, Western caution about taking on burdens to the east, and these countries' poor track record on reform. In-Betweens Armenia and Belarus, along with Kazakhstan, opted to throw in more or less wholeheartedly with Russia. For the other In-Betweens, the unpalatability of sticking with Moscow, and the lack of an option of prompt entry into the Western tent, reduced them to coexisting with Russia and, when practicable, balancing against it, even in cases when segments of their elites would have been happier following the East Central Europeans and bandwagoning with an ascendant West. The elites as a rule had no appetite, however, for decisive market reform and democratic governance, Polish-style, or for relinquishing the political monopoly and lucrative economic rents that went with the status quo. Public opinion, which did not always mimic elite opinion, was still another constraint. In Ukraine, for example, citizens in 2000 had a much warmer view of Russia than of the US or NATO, and 60% approved of an East Slavic confederation with Russia and Belarus.[78]

In practice, restrained balancing against Russia could work in an assortment of tangible ways, rarely earth-shaking. In expeditions to the post-Soviet capitals, Western envoys got used to hearing pleas to intercede with Moscow on their behalf, on points both petty and consequential. Few meetings passed without requests for public manifestations of solidarity with the locals. Governments enrolled in all available international organisations, signed declarations of good wishes ad infinitum with the Americans and Europeans, garnered invitations to Brussels, Berlin and Washington, showed up at protocol events and celebrations staged by the West, and dragged their feet on the implementation of CIS agreements. They could also accept or solicit sometimes-generous Western foreign-aid programmes. These were ostensibly apolitical measures but they reflected the realities of the time: Western prosperity and Russia's relative lack of resources. From 1995 onwards, the US had a declared policy to give the In-Betweens and the Central Asians a bigger collective slice of the assistance pie for the former Soviet region than Russia's share. By 1998, Russia received only 17% of the total aid for the 12 post-Soviet Eurasian countries, while Ukraine, with less than one-third of Russia's population, got more and was now the third-largest recipient after Israel and Egypt globally. 'In part, strategic considerations – including the desire to fortify the security and independence of Ukraine and Uzbekistan and the goal of establishing better relations with the oil-rich states of the Caspian region – pushed aid in this non-Russian direction.'[79] Pocketing favours from one side was not seen as incompatible with doing the same from the other. Some of the In-Between leaders of the time – Kuchma of Ukraine and Shevardnadze of Georgia come to mind – were virtuosos at playing the West and Russia off each other in order to wring concessions from both.

An oft-heard explanation of the turbulence between Russia and the West that eventually surfaced is the coming to power of a new Russian president: Vladimir Putin, inaugurated in May 2000 after serving four months as acting president following Yeltsin's early retirement. In fact, Putin's arrival corresponded with several years of an upturn, generally speaking, in Russian interaction with the West. The new man in the Kremlin revived the NATO–Russia relationship and received the NATO secretary-general, George Robertson, soon after taking office. The latter opined that things had crept 'from the permafrost into slightly softer ground'.[80] Putin's public statements recalled Yeltsin's and Gorbachev's musings about Russia finding a home in the Western community. 'Russia', he said in an interview with David Frost of the BBC in 2000, 'is part of the European culture', and he could not picture it 'in isolation from Europe and what we often call the civilised world'. He was against demonising NATO as a perpetual enemy; 'even posing the question this way will not do any good to Russia or the world'. 'Could Russia ever join NATO?', Frost wanted to know. 'I don't see why not', replied Putin. 'I would not rule out such a possibility … if and when Russia's views are taken into account as those of an equal partner.'[81] He raised the issue of Russia's potential NATO membership when he first met an American president, Bill Clinton, in June 2000. Clinton was non-committal, but Kremlin staffers were instructed to investigate the nuts and bolts of Russian accession.[82] Putin hit it off personally with several Western leaders, including Clinton's successor, George W. Bush. After meeting the Russian in Slovenia in June 2001, Bush legendarily exclaimed that he had caught a glimpse of Putin's 'soul'.

Putin telephoned Bush with condolences over the 9/11 attacks before any other world leader, and asked CIS governments in Central Asia to satisfy US basing needs for the onslaught against al-Qaeda and the Taliban in Afghanistan. Russia filled intelligence gaps before the American invasion and there was some cooperation with the American services in the field. This led to talk of a new US–Russia alliance in the war on terror. In the months after 9/11, Putin again raised the possibility of a Russian place in NATO with Robertson. The NATO secretary-general reportedly gave him the standard line about formal procedures and practices. Putin undoubtedly heard: 'get in line behind Estonia and Bulgaria'.

A decidedly more forward American posture in post-Soviet Eurasia – in part a by-product of the Bush administration's global prioritisation of counter-terrorism and democracy promotion – chipped away at the Clinton-era tradition of self-imposed restraints and consideration of Russian sensitivities. In the spring of 2002, for example, Washington embarked on the Georgia Train and Equip Program (GTEP), spending some US$65m and sending in several hundred US special forces to participate. It was designed to modernise the Georgian military and get into shape four battle-ready battalions that could do their bit in the war on terror. The immediate assignment was to pacify the restive Pankisi Gorge abutting the Russian republic of Chechnya, where a war against separatists was raging. Putin mouthed tentative support (his government had long complained about Chechen rebels taking refuge in Pankisi), but Russian attitudes cooled once new projects replaced GTEP and Georgian forces were enlisted in the American adventure in Iraq. 'The minuscule U.S. presence in Georgia had a symbolic significance far greater than was warranted by its size, and presaged a trend that became increasingly visible during the decade and increasingly worrisome to Moscow.'[83]

Also reflective of lowered inhibitions was the American decision to build a bridge to the Russo-sceptic GUAM group. In December 2002 the US and the GUAM foreign ministers entered into a framework programme 'of trade and transport facilitation, ensuring border and customs control, combating terrorism, organized crime and drug trafficking'. The centrepiece was a US-bankrolled GUAM Virtual Center designed to conduct activities along these lines. The financial commitment was trifling, and the impact even more so, but that did not keep Russia from seeing it as a suspicious probe.[84]

One effect of this US policy shift was to embolden Russia's neighbours to bid more overtly for Western support and for inclusion in Western institutions. A pair of In-Betweens blazed a declaratory trail toward the EU and even NATO, where Russian tolerance for deviation from the status quo would certainly be scantiest. In 1998 Ukraine's president Kuchma asserted EU membership as a strategic objective, and in 2002 let it be known that he wanted his country sooner or later to join the NATO alliance; Shevardnadze staked similar claims for Georgia in 1999 and 2002, respectively.

In a third country, Moldova, a bruising scandal broke out in 2003 over resolution of the Transnistria conflict. At the invitation of the Moldovan president, Vladimir Voronin, a senior adviser to Putin, Dmitry Kozak, drafted with local allies a plan to bring the mutinous district back into the fold by adopting a new federal constitution for the country. The Kozak Memorandum would have resulted in an asymmetric federation; Transnistria and Gagauzia (the small homeland of a Turkic-speaking people) were to be granted considerable autonomy along with a veto over some central decisions via a new upper house of parliament. In a late addition, Russian peacekeepers, and not the multinational force the Moldovan authorities preferred, were to be stationed in Transnistria until 2020. Western officials, prominently Javier Solana, the EU's high representative for common foreign and security policy, were vehemently against the plan, while OSCE mediators could not arrive at a position. Voronin, having given preliminary approval to the scheme, torpedoed it in November 2003. His decision came as a Kremlin airplane was preparing to ferry Putin to Chisinau to witness the signing. As William Hill, then the head of the OSCE mission to Moldova, later recalled, 'What was for most Western capitals a relatively minor incident for the Russians was a personal affront to their president and a denial of Russia's right to play an independent political and diplomatic role in a part of the world that had once been theirs exclusively.'[85]

For Moscow, unease over Western involvement in the debacle in Moldova turned into alarm when taken together with trends in several other nearby states. Georgia, Ukraine – the premier In-Between, and Kyrgyzstan were rattled around this time by 'colour revolutions' propelled by mass protest and civil resistance. The three revolutions came within 18 months: the Rose Revolution in Georgia in November 2003, which unseated Shevardnadze; the Orange Revolution in Ukraine in

December 2004, after a disputed national election to replace Kuchma, which denied the presidency to Kuchma's associate, Viktor Yanukovych; and, in April 2005, the Tulip Revolution in Kyrgyzstan, in which perennial leader Askar Akaev fell from power. The events in Bishkek, Kyrgyzstan, were reminiscent of those in Tbilisi and Kyiv but otherwise had scant international resonance. The same could not be said of the Rose and Orange revolutions. Shevardnadze and Kuchma had thumbed their noses at Russia on NATO, but they had been senior members of the Soviet *nomenklatura*, and Kuchma had played along with Russia's SES initiative. Their replacements – Mikheil Saakashvili and Viktor Yushchenko – were pro-Western nationalists who would necessarily be more of a handful for Moscow. Russia played go-between in Georgia but in Ukraine unabashedly took Yanukovych's side, with Putin making two well-publicised visits to Kyiv during the election campaign, the Kremlin paying for pro-Yanukovych polling and electoral activities, and a premature congratulatory phone call from Putin to Yanukovych after the disputed second-round vote. American and European democracy-promotion programmes had funded some of the non-governmental organisations (NGOs) and movements that swept Saakashvili and Yushchenko into office; Western governments and media effusively embraced the new governments. That was enough for Russian officials to dismiss them as lapdogs of the West, and above all of the US, which Putin indicted for a high-handed foreign policy boxed in 'beautiful, pseudo-democratic phraseology'.[86]

The interactions described hitherto added up to a messy equilibrium among the main external actors in post-Soviet Eurasia. In time, the equilibrium was revealed to be fragile. The Cold Peace got colder and the interaction in the region more and more unmistakably adversarial. Discord erupted with greater frequency, at a shriller pitch and with more animosity.

CHAPTER TWO

Contestation entrenched

A decade and a half after the settlement-that-wasn't marked the end of the Cold War, the best opportunity to forge a new, inclusive order for Europe and Eurasia had passed. The year 2004 brought the 'big bang' enlargement of Euro-Atlantic institutions, ushering the Baltic states and several adjacent countries into NATO and the EU.[1] The Western umbrella now extended deep into the former imperium of the Soviet Union. But at that time one could find only hints of the ferociously adversarial behaviour that yielded a hot war in Ukraine a decade later. Russia was far from happy with what had transpired since 1989, and often exuded resentment. Yet it had a multilayered and interdependent relationship with the EU and its member states, a functional dialogue with the US and even some cooperation with NATO. Although Moscow was on guard about Western activity in post-Soviet Eurasia, the competition was still low-grade in comparison with today.

A few short years after the colour revolutions, tensions over geopolitics and geo-ideas reached unheard-of levels, a process that culminated in a five-day war between Russia and Georgia in August 2008. The focus then moved to geo-economics, as the

EU became more active and Russia finally got serious about its plans for regional economic integration. While contingent factors temporarily eased tensions during the 'reset' interval, contestation had now been entrenched.

The Cold Peace unravels

The tenuous and mostly informal arrangement in post-Soviet Eurasia that emerged from the 1990s had reflected Russia's relative dominance in the region, constraints on Russia–West competition, and a shared sense that Russian institutions and practices were gradually converging with Western ones. Vladimir Putin, in his first few years in power, subscribed, at least rhetorically, to the logic of convergence, but by 2003–04 he was moving the Russian political system down a more authoritarian path. The ponderings of officials and intellectuals (Western and Russian alike) about the eventual drawing of Russia into the West's institutional web had not yet died out, but they were looking more and more implausible.

But it was the colour revolutions of 2003–05, and most of all Ukraine's Orange Revolution in 2004, that truly kicked off the unravelling of the Cold Peace. Breakdowns of regimes that were part of the status quo order in the region testified to a waning of Russian influence. The instinct of Russia and the West to respond to these breakdowns in opposite and opposing ways also pointed to more hard-hitting competition on the horizon.

The colour revolutions solidified linkages between geopolitics and geo-ideas in the region. Moscow came around to the interpretation that the uprisings next door were a tool of Western, and pointedly of American, policy. The tool was deployed, many in positions of authority argued, in order to remove sitting governments that pursued policies counter to US interests, replace them with figures who would do the Americans' bidding, or conceivably, if all else failed, to sow sheer disorder. According to this view, colour revolutions were particularly insidious because they furthered power objectives under the cover of devotion to universal principles of democracy and human rights – what the Russians call *maskirovka* (camouflage). The West's geo-ideas, in short, were geopolitics in disguise.[2] The Russian military developed a detailed schematic for this purported policy, beginning with Western government sponsorship of efforts to train opposition movements, moving to the process of delegitimising sitting governments, sparking protests and so on until the final act of installation of a puppet regime.[3]

Incongruities abounded in the Russian narrative. We mention just three here. Firstly, the popular uprisings in question originated predominantly in domestic outrage about poor governance, not intrigues by foreigners. Secondly, they occurred under a tangle of circumstances and led to very different outcomes. In Georgia, Russia was far more involved in mediating the political crisis than any Western country. In Kyrgyzstan, the successor government under Kurmanbek Bakiev behaved no differently toward Russia or the West than the *ancien régime*. In Ukraine (see below), Western-sounding rhetoric outpaced Western-tending policy. Thirdly, the degree of Western involvement in the uprisings and the extent to which Washington in particular guided the aftermath was grossly overstated.

The blemishes and blinkers in the Russian narrative are beside the point. Threat perceptions do not need to be logically consistent; they matter to the extent that they are widely held in a country's political establishment. It became a consensus view in Moscow that the West, beginning with the United States, was fomenting colour revolutions in post-Soviet Eurasia as a non-kinetic means of engineering the same result as *Operation Iraqi Freedom* did in Iraq: regime change. And, to be fair, there were kernels of truth in the Russian narrative. The US and the EU did provide training to some of the activists and parties that came to power as a result of the revolutions, and often were involved in brokering political compromises.[4] Moreover, some US officials did claim credit for these events, although sometimes the very same individuals would also downplay the American role.[5] And in the cases of the Rose and Orange revolutions, as well as in later upheavals in the region, the governments that emerged were indisputably more pro-Western, loosely speaking, than their predecessors. In Ukraine, president Yushchenko and Yulia Tymoshenko, his co-revolutionary prime minister, had for some time been proponents of NATO and EU membership and opposed closer ties with Russia. When they came to power, there truly was a swing in Ukrainian foreign policy. Kuchma had attempted to balance between Russia and the West so as to maximise benefits; the new government tacked sharply toward the West.

Domestic politics in the region had thus become an arena of Russia–West contestation. It was a matter of geo-ideas as much as geopolitics. For Moscow, the struggle was linked to preservation of domestic stability, since it was widely taken as gospel truth that political change in the neighbourhood could be used to undermine the foundations of the Russian government. For the West, the colour revolutions also solidified a linkage between geopolitics and geo-ideas. 'Pro-Western' became synonymous with 'democratic' as a descriptor of local political forces. Democratic political change and geopolitical gain went hand in hand, and many saw Russia as an impediment to both.

This mode of thinking was quite familiar to many Western policymakers: in East Central Europe, democratisation and market reforms had coincided with geopolitical realignment in their favour. The circumstances of post-Soviet Eurasia were markedly different, and the assumed linkage with geo-ideas often led Western policy astray. In the end, none of the colour revolutions was a genuine democratic breakthrough.[6] Kyrgyzstan, which was little involved in the Russia–West tussle, was more repressive under Bakiev than it had been under Akaev, and in 2010 Bakiev was to be overthrown much like his predecessor. Post-Orange Revolution Ukraine was less repressive than under Kuchma, but its leaders were anything but democratic exemplars, often behaving quite similarly to their predecessors. Many corrupt practices continued unabated, and precious little was done to establish the rule of law. In Georgia, governance under Saakashvili's administration did make impressive strides, especially in terms of anti-corruption policy, but pluralism and human rights did not. Any illusions should have been put to rest by a crackdown on protesters and subsequent takeover of the country's main independent television station in November 2007. While the West often claimed to be shunning authoritarian regimes for their authoritarianism, not infrequently, as with Georgia in 2007, it overlooked the democratic shortcomings of governments that vowed their loyalty.[7]

In the years following the colour revolutions, Russia moved towards a counter-revolutionary regional policy. This has been widely misconstrued as a drive to sabotage democratic norms.[8] The evidence to support such claims is thin. Russian policymakers, whose cynicism often seems to know no bounds, do not see their neighbourhood principally through an ideological lens. Their objective instead is to have *druzhestvennye* (friendly) neighbours, that is, states whose leaders are not hostile to Russia. How these leaders get to power and how their political institutions function is of little concern. As one of us has written, 'Russia has been more indifferent to authoritarianism in its former empire – homegrown, for the most part – than avidly supportive of it. There is no systematic correspondence between regime type and the relationship with Russia.'[9] Moscow's counter-revolutionary turn was driven by the notion that revolutionary change had become a Western implement to undermine Russian interests. Moscow could no longer distinguish (what the West couched as) democratic change from loss of influence. Geopolitics and geo-ideas were now hopelessly entangled. As events were to demonstrate, the mix was highly combustible.

But Moscow does not have an authoritarianism-promotion agenda, an analogue to EU and US democracy promotion. Any policy of norm promotion is predicated not only on affirmative preferences but on deployment of the means to achieve them. Russia demonstrates neither.[10] The broader point here is that a simple dichotomy between a West altruistically promoting democratic norms and a Russia deliberately supporting authoritarianism does not match reality. By this period, a three-front regional competition – in geopolitics, geo-economics and geo-ideas – was central to decision-making on *both* sides.

Moscow's immediate reaction to the Orange Revolution was relatively mild. Clearly, it was not pleased either by the revolutionary form of political change or by the ascendance of a leadership with an inimical policy agenda. But Putin did not attempt to isolate the Orange leaders. Yushchenko was invited to visit Moscow in February 2005, and Putin reciprocated with a trip to Kyiv the next month, meeting both Yushchenko and Tymoshenko, who seemed to be jostling for his favour.[11] The presidential meeting produced an agreement to create a Putin–Yushchenko Commission to oversee various mid-level working groups, and approval of a work plan for the year.

The new government in Kyiv did not pull out of Russia's favoured integration format of the moment, the SES, continuing Kuchma's approach of protracted talks with minimal firm commitments. At the time, Russia held out the prospect that joining the SES and pursuing European integration need not be irreconcilable. As Putin said during his visit to Kyiv in March 2005, 'The statement that the SES involves movement in one direction, while cooperation with the EU entails movement in the opposite direction, is totally false.' He went on to describe the plans for creating the Four Common Spaces with the EU, one of which was a common economic space – 'essentially, the harmonisation of Russian and EU laws', as Putin put it. If Moscow and Kyiv work together toward that end, that would 'create the preconditions' for Ukraine's 'movement toward Europe'.[12] Indeed, at that time Russia's economic coordination with the EU was more advanced than Ukraine's. The EU had much more of a donor–recipient relationship with Kyiv; a 2004 European Commission report highlights the EU's status as the largest donor to Ukraine and discusses future integration only notionally.[13] An analogous Commission document on the relationship with Russia describes a plan to create a shared 'open and integrated market' between the two, specifying a range of steps including common standardisation for industrial products, intellectual-property regulation, competition policies and regulatory convergence.[14]

Yet the Kremlin was not prepared to subsidise a Ukrainian government that was now actively pursuing NATO and EU membership, while only paying lip service to Russia's integration agenda. World oil prices were hitting new highs at the time, driving up the price European customers paid to Gazprom, the Russian state-controlled energy giant, for natural gas. The real value of the implicit subsidy Russia provided to Ukraine shot up as a result, and with it the opportunity cost of maintaining the practice. By the end of 2005, Ukraine was paying up to four times less for gas than Gazprom's European customers.[15]

Without an incentive to do favours for the new government in Kyiv, the Kremlin was unwilling to order Gazprom to forfeit market prices on exports to Ukraine. During the negotiations over renewal of the supply contract in late 2005, Gazprom accordingly sought to cancel subsidised pricing unless Kyiv agreed to a consortium arrangement for its pipeline network. Kyiv turned Gazprom down, and threatened to divert to Ukrainian consumers gas meant for Europe if no compromise were to be found. On 1 January 2006, Russia interrupted supplies to Ukraine after the deadline had passed; it back-pedalled quickly after Ukraine started siphoning off gas meant for the EU and pressure dropped in several European countries. An arrangement was reached empowering a shady intermediary, RosUkrEnergo, to manage the bilateral gas relationship, which enriched well-connected elites in Moscow and Kyiv alike.

Breathless press coverage at the time portrayed Russia's actions as the use of gas as a political weapon. The reality was more complex. Ending munificent subsidies can scarcely be portrayed as punishment, and it was unclear what political objective Russia might have been pursuing, besides alienating EU and Ukrainian publics and elites. A more cogent explanation is that Russia was moving to a two-pronged approach to the issue of gas exports to its neighbours: cheap gas only for countries willing to participate in its integration projects and to share ownership of gas assets; unsentimental commercial terms for the rest. In early 2006 only Belarus, which joined every Russia-led grouping and ceded control of its gas monopoly to Gazprom, avoided a price hike.

The first Russia–Ukraine gas war was a demonstration of Moscow's quickness to resort to economic duress whenever it perceives a neighbour to be misbehaving. More often than not, such tactics have boomeranged. Even when they induced short-term compliance, the long-term cost of loss of trust and goodwill, especially given historically conditioned threat perceptions, outweighed the gains. Russian policy toward the region has rarely taken into account such sensitivities.

Moscow continued its coercive economic diplomacy in the region throughout the subsequent years. The motives, as far as one can divine from the circumstances, ranged from punishment for perceived bad behaviour to strong-arming concessions during unrelated negotiations. Moscow rarely announced its objectives openly, instead airing ludicrous cover stories for public consumption. In 2006 alone, allegations of hygiene violations led to import bans on dairy, meat and poultry products from Ukraine (January); Georgian and Moldovan wine (March); and Georgian mineral water (May). Later that year, in retaliation for the Georgians' public arrest of four suspected Russian spies, Moscow suspended all transportation links with Georgia, and deported migrant workers amidst what seemed to be a campaign of intimidation against ethnic Georgians in Russia. There were two energy disputes with Belarus in 2006–07, including an oil cut-off. Little by way of grand design seems to have been involved. As Rilka Dragneva and Kataryna Wolczuk note, Moscow had developed a reflex of 'deploying selective, targeted sanctions toward any states which pursued a policy that Russia regarded as unfriendly'.[16] The tactical goals varied in these scattered episodes. Taken together, the Russian actions did not amount to much, let alone a strategy for regional domination.

What is often called Russian soft power in its neighbourhood became a focus in the period following the colour revolutions. But Joseph Nye's classic definition of soft power – the 'ability to get what you want through attraction rather than through coercion' – never quite fit the Russian case. Less than two months after the Orange Revolution, Putin established a 'department for inter-regional and cultural ties with foreign countries' in the presidential administration, with a mission to solidify the bonds with former Soviet neighbours. Its first director was Modest Kolerov, the founder of the news site Regnum, which had a well-honed anti-Western bent and a focus on those same neighbours. Pro-Russian NGOs sprouted across the region, including in sensitive areas like Transnistria and Crimea. Groups of this ilk organised protests that disrupted a planned NATO–Ukraine exercise in the Crimean port of Feodosia in 2006. Assertions of Russian government funding for the NGOs throughout the region were ubiquitous in Western analysis. The evidence offered was circumstantial at best. A dearth of hard data is part of the problem: some groups certainly received financing from Russia, but the very opacity of these arrangements suggested a sinister intent, sharpening threat perceptions. Even though Moscow's actions bore some likeness to common Western soft-power instruments, they lacked transparency and featured ominous undertones. It was more like 'soft coercion', as James Sherr puts it, than soft power.[17] Even efforts to engage Russian co-ethnics in the region seemed underhanded.[18]

The colour revolutions helped catalyse a tough Western, particularly American, approach to the region. In Washington, a well-placed faction within and around the Bush administration was determined to continue the enlargement of Euro-Atlantic institutions. Its most high-ranking member was then-vice president Dick Cheney, who, as he was to write in his memoir, 'had long believed that the United States should play a more active role in integrating Ukraine and other former Soviet states into the West'.[19] It also included some figures who had been at the forefront of the first round of NATO enlargement. One of them, Ronald Asmus, explicitly argued in 2005 that:

> the Orange Revolution has opened up an opportunity to redraw the map of Europe and Eurasia. ...

> Anchoring Central and Eastern Europe to the West
> was a tremendous strategic accomplishment. ... The
> Orange Revolution has now offered us the historic
> chance to extend that same degree of peace and stabil-
> ity further eastward into Ukraine, perhaps across the
> Black Sea and maybe eventually into Russia itself.
> ... Ukraine's anchoring to the West must become the
> next step in the completion of Europe and the Euro-
> Atlantic community.

He anticipated that Ukraine could be granted a NATO Membership Action Plan 'no later than the next NATO summit in 2006'.[20] For this group, expanding NATO's writ had become intimately linked to democracy promotion. Bush himself writes in his memoir, 'I viewed NATO expansion as a powerful tool to advance the freedom agenda.'[21]

The period of largely unchallenged Russian predominance among the outside actors in the region had clearly come to an end. The fuse had thus been lit for an explosion. An ambitious agenda to seize the moment following the colour revolutions was taking hold in certain Western capitals. This agenda – and the conflation of nominal democratisation, as touted by geo-ideas, with geopolitical gain – was amplified by the new leaders in Kyiv and Tbilisi, who were far more savvy about getting their message across in the West than their predecessors. Incendiary rhetoric heightened Russian paranoia about Western intentions. In May 2006, Cheney delivered a speech in Vilnius, Lithuania, in which he said: 'The system that has brought such great hope to the shores of the Baltic can bring the same hope to the far shores of the Black Sea, and beyond. What is true in Vilnius is also true in Tbilisi and Kiev, and true in Minsk, and true in Moscow.'[22] One can only conjecture the reaction to such statements in the Kremlin.

Yet there was no consensus in the West about extending offers of formal membership to the new aspirants in post-Soviet Eurasia. In NATO, one of the reasons cited by those member states opposed to such a step for Ukraine was the lack of popular support for membership.[23] So the Bush administration pushed the Ukrainian authorities 'to become more actively involved in the public outreach and education campaign about NATO and why it is in Ukraine's national interest to join the Alliance'.[24] Washington was thus going far beyond support for Ukraine's aspirations, as it often claimed. It was selectively reading those aspirations, focusing on parts of the elite and not the public, and attempting to alter them.

The Bush administration also threw more support than before behind the GUAM enterprise. It came in the form of high-level participation in US–GUAM meetings and a significant hike in financial support.[25] It is hard not to read US assistance to the grouping as anything other than an attempt to strengthen intra-regional ties that did not involve Russia.

The accumulated tensions began to take their toll on the regional security architecture. At the OSCE summit in Istanbul in November 1999, an Agreement on Adaptation of the Treaty on Conventional Armed Forces in Europe (A/CFE) had been signed, modernising the 1990 treaty as a confidence- and security-building measure for the post-Cold War environment. At the same summit, Moscow made commitments to withdraw its remaining military units in Georgia (in stages) and Moldova (by the end of 2002). Moscow ratified the new treaty, which it much preferred to the original, but slow-rolled the withdrawal commitments. NATO member states in 2002 adopted a policy of formally linking their ratification of A/CFE to Russia's following through on its commitments. By 2003, the annual OSCE summits, the NATO–Russia Council (a consultative body established in 2002) and CFE implementation meetings were marred by polemics between Russia and the West about what came to be known as the Istanbul Commitments. The removal of troops from Moldova came to a halt in March 2004 and has never resumed. Russian forces had left Georgia by November 2007.[26] By that time, though, the CFE regime at large was on the verge of implosion.

Russia had dug in its heels in Moldova following the collapse of the Kozak Memorandum and Russian-inspired settlement efforts in 2003. But the West, and particularly the US, seemed intent on using the linkage between A/CFE ratification and the Istanbul Commitments to drive Russia's army out of the region and force settlements to the protracted conflicts. In Moldova, Russia's military presence was twofold: remnants of the 14th Army guarding weapons stockpiles, and the Russian component of the peacekeeping force (PKF), created via the ceasefire deal that terminated the fighting in Transnistria in 1992. Within NATO, no ally questioned that the Istanbul Commitments governed the former, but the latter was the subject of dispute. The US insisted there was a link and proposed to replace the PKF with a multinational EU–Russia force.[27] Washington's position on this issue seemed designed to compel Moscow to accept terms regarding the Transnistria conflict and its presence there by holding back on A/CFE ratification, which Moscow was eager to achieve. The gambit backfired.

In April 2007, Putin, in his annual address to parliament, declared a moratorium on Russia's implementation of the original CFE agreement, evidently in order to force NATO to ratify A/CFE. He denounced Western 'attempts to gain unilateral advantages' by 'making use of an invented pretext for not ratifying [A/CFE]' while 'build[ing] up their own system of military bases along our borders'.[28] In December of that year, Russia suspended its implementation of CFE, while no NATO member state moved to ratify A/CFE.[29]

This incident epitomised the ruinous character of the hardening regional contestation. Both Russia and the West adopted inflexible zero-sum stances regarding a dispute on regional security and were prepared to cling to them rather than negotiate a compromise solution. In the end, Russia's attempt to force NATO member states to ratify A/CFE had failed, and the West had made no progress on the frozen conflicts. Everyone lost the transparency and accountability of the original CFE, and Moldova missed a chance to rid itself of an unwanted Russian military presence.

No more Yaltas

The demise of the conventional arms-control regime fed an upsurge in tensions between Russia and the West in 2007–08. Putin's speech at the Munich security conference in February 2007, in which he pilloried various aspects of US foreign policy, set the tone. The tensions deepened in February 2008 when Kosovo declared its independence from Serbia and was recognised by the US and most of its European allies. Russia was bitterly opposed, and warned that diplomatic acknowledgement of Kosovo's independence would have ramifications for the unrecognised entities in post-Soviet Eurasia. In the interim, another dispute had broken out regarding the prospect of a NATO Membership Action Plan (MAP) for Ukraine and Georgia.

Introduced in 1999, MAP was an obscure bureaucratic step for aspirants to NATO membership, setting down the conditions required to join. A MAP did not imply automatic membership of NATO, as the final decision on a candidate nation's accession was to be a political one, requiring a unanimous vote among the allies. In the heat of the tensions of 2008, though, both Russian and Western officials treated MAP as tantamount to NATO membership and adopted equally inflexible positions. In February 2008, a Russian deputy foreign minister warned the US ambassador in Moscow that 'Russia would not consider a MAP offer as a "technical" step. It would be a strategic challenge with serious strategic consequences. … [It] would affect not only Russia–Ukraine and Russia–Georgia relations but also Russia's partnership with the US.'[30] Such statements fed the pro-MAP drive in Washington. As then-secretary of state Condoleezza Rice recalls, 'For the West, given the pressures that Moscow had been placing on Georgia, Mikheil Saakashvili's government had a good claim for the MAP as a counterweight to Russia.'[31] MAP had become the primary gauge of the larger contestation in the region.

The denouement would come at the NATO summit in Bucharest, Romania, in April 2008. In the months leading up to that meeting, the MAP question had become highly contentious within NATO; allies were divided between opponents, led by Germany and France, and ardent supporters, including East Central European states and the US. For supporters, the issue had become a litmus test for willingness to take on Russia's influence in Georgia, Ukraine and post-Soviet Eurasia more broadly. As Asmus writes, advocates of MAP were 'not necessarily interested in the details of whether Georgia had or had not successfully completed all of its reforms'. Instead, 'they believed it was necessary to embrace and reassure Georgia at this critical moment when so much seemed to hang in the balance, and to send a message to Moscow to back off.'[32]

The Bush administration pressed the case for MAP publicly during the president's visit to Ukraine, en route to Bucharest. At a joint press conference with Yushchenko, Bush said, 'Your nation has made a bold decision [to request a MAP], and the United States strongly supports your request. In Bucharest this week, I will continue to make America's position clear: We support MAP for Ukraine and Georgia.' He added that he had recently said the same to Putin in a phone conversation, telling him, 'you shouldn't fear that, Mr President. I mean, after all, NATO is [an] organization that's peaceful, or NATO is an organization that helps democracies flourish. Democracies are good things to have on your border.'[33] Putin and his advisers did not view this development in similarly rosy geo-ideational terms.

It is rare that NATO summits involve substantive negotiations over important issues. Working-level officials in allied governments usually hash out all the agreements weeks beforehand, making the summits largely ceremonial occasions at which the leaders provide their blessing to the already-agreed texts. Bucharest was different; there was no consensus on MAP for Georgia and Ukraine. The debate at the foreign-minister level demonstrated changes to the intra-Alliance dynamic from a particular source – admission of the ten new members from East Central Europe in 1999 and 2004. When the German foreign minister voiced reservations about MAP, he was shouted down by his Polish colleague, who said that '[MAP] is a matter of national security for us. And now you come and tell us you are more worried for Moscow than for your allies.'[34] In the end, heads of state and government negotiated an ad hoc compromise: no MAP, but the summit communiqué declared that Ukraine and Georgia 'will become' members of NATO at some unspecified future point.[35] Never before had NATO promised membership to aspirant states. The beleaguered leaders were making a necessary compromise to avoid a diplomatic meltdown. But once the parley was over it became clear that the decision was the worst of all worlds: while providing no increased security to Ukraine and Georgia, the Bucharest Declaration reinforced the view in Moscow that NATO was determined to incorporate them at any cost.

Bucharest also marked the breakdown of NATO's dual-track approach to enlargement and relations with Russia: pursuing new members while also fashioning a more wide-ranging partnership with Moscow, as enshrined in the 1997 Founding Act. The evening following the release of the declaration, Putin arrived in the Romanian capital for a scheduled NATO–Russia summit. His public comments made clear Russia's bottom line: 'the appearance of a powerful military bloc' on its borders was 'a direct threat' to its security. 'The claim that this process is not directed against Russia will not suffice.'[36] The State Duma, the lower house of the Russian parliament, was soon to pass a resolution urging the abrogation of the 1997 Russia–Ukraine treaty, which had reaffirmed Ukraine's territorial integrity, if Kyiv received a MAP.

In remarks to the NATO leaders behind closed doors, Putin made clear that Russia still did not consider its neighbours to be real countries entitled to their own policies. Georgia, he said, was foolhardy to think that NATO membership would resolve its separatist conflicts. He also called Ukraine an artificial creation of capricious Soviet leaders.[37] (Putin's characterisation, of course, was by the same token true of post-Soviet Russia, which had never existed in its current borders before 1991.)

Such statements increasingly made it taboo for Western governments to hold any discussions with Moscow about post-Soviet Eurasia. Partly this came out of the Bush administration's (and its supporters') peculiar reading of mid-twentieth-century diplomacy. In his maiden speech in Europe in June 2001, Bush said, 'We will not trade away the fate of free European peoples. No more Munichs, no more Yaltas.'[38] He was equating the Yalta accord, signed by the Big Three at the end of the Second World War, with Munich in 1938, the archetype of a sell-out of help-less countries to odious regimes. It should be noted that this characterisation is tendentious if not ahistorical; the Red Army had occupied most of East Central Europe when the Yalta agreement was signed.[39] Whatever the historical accuracy, Yalta now signified the granting of carte blanche to Stalin to impose tyrannical regimes fashioned in the Soviet image on the states of East Central Europe – a Western sin that must never be repeated. The invocation of the Yalta analogy implied that cooperation with Moscow would necessitate imposing decisions on Russia's neighbours against their will, depriving them of democracy, independence and so on. When the East Central European states that had experienced the trauma of Yalta joined Euro-Atlantic institutions, this idea gained broader currency. But it was Putin's words, and Russian policy broadly speaking, that crystallised that view into conventional wisdom.

Another geo-ideational conflict was brewing. Bush said in his June 2001 speech that it was not just immoral to find common ground with Russia on the regional order, as per the 'no more Yaltas' maxim; additionally, the president reinterpreted 'what my father called a Europe whole and free' as a concrete policy agenda. 'All of Europe's new democracies, from the Baltic to the Black Sea and all that lie between, should have the same chance for security and freedom and the same chance to join the institutions of Europe as Europe's old democracies have.' Suddenly, for the continent to be 'whole and free' (for good measure, 'at peace' soon became part of the trope), every country had to join the Western club. To be precise, every country save one: 'Europe's great institutions – NATO and the European Union – can and should build partnerships with Russia', but not more than that.[40] As Russia gained seriousness of purpose about its regional-integration agenda, thus giving the In-Betweens alternative club membership options, the geo-idea of a 'Europe whole, free and at peace' began to collide with the other Western favourite: freedom to choose. If a country were to choose to join a Russia-led club, presumably Europe would not be whole or free, and maybe not even at peace.

A frozen conflict heats up

As the politicians huddled in Bucharest, the security situation in the South Caucasus was going downhill. In the weeks
following the recognition of Kosovo's independence, Moscow
publicly reached out to the small, unrecognised breakaway entities within Georgia, South Ossetia and Abkhazia, seemingly in
order to demonstrate its pique at the Kosovo decision. Between
early March and mid-April, the government announced it
would no longer be bound by a 1996 CIS decision limiting
trade with Abkhazia; the Duma passed a non-binding resolution calling for recognition of the enclaves' independence; and
Putin issued a decree opening up greater trade, transportation
and political links with both places. These steps were primarily
symbolic; the CIS sanctions had never been enforced, and links
between Russia and the two separatist regions had always
existed. But they caused panic in Tbilisi, leading many there to
assume that Russia was marching toward annexation.[41]

The Georgian government responded by bolstering its
military presence near Abkhazia and conducting more drone
flights over the region. In hectic succession, a Russian MiG-29
shot down several drones, there was a rancorous UN Security
Council meeting on the issue and Russia boosted its peacekeeping forces in Abkhazia. Communication had broken down, and
political will to defuse the situation was absent. When the chief
of the Russian general staff warned his NATO counterparts in
May that there would be a war in Georgia that summer unless
steps were taken to nip it in the bud, 'NATO thought it was just
standard Russian bluster and political posturing'.[42]

As the summer arrived, South Ossetia became the eye of
the storm, with numerous skirmishes between Georgian and
separatist forces, while Russia conducted a 10,000-man military exercise just across the border, ending on 2 August. What
came next has been well documented by an international fact-

finding mission on the conflict.[43] Following an intensification of fighting, on the night of 7 August Saakashvili took the fateful decision to unleash an all-out assault on Tskhinvali, the South Ossetian provincial capital. The Russian peacekeepers there also came under direct attack. Russia, after being caught flat-footed, launched a massive counter-offensive, not only driving the Georgians (both armed forces and ethnic Georgian civilians) out of South Ossetia but pushing deep into Tbilisi-governed territory, gratuitously sinking several of Georgia's naval vessels after the fighting had ended (and hauling off patrol boats as trophies), and destroying much of the hardware of the country's ground forces. Russian forces also invaded across the administrative boundary with Abkhazia, which Georgia had not attacked, and dismantled or destroyed a number of military facilities. In five days, the war was over; Saakashvili had been routed. An estimated 500 people had been killed, and tens of thousands had been displaced. On 26 August, the recently instated Russian president, Dmitry Medvedev, recognised the independence of South Ossetia and Abkhazia.

Prevailing interpretations of the conflict – either Saakashvili fell into an elaborate Russian trap or he launched a murderous *Reconquista* war with a tacit green light from Washington – are equally fallacious. Both assume premeditation and planning that the facts do not corroborate. It does look as if the Georgian government had been gearing up for a war, but earlier in the summer, and in Abkhazia, not South Ossetia.[44] In the hours leading up to the decision to attack, the Georgian leadership seemed to have come to believe that a Russian invasion was in motion.[45] Russia may well have been trying to provoke Saakashvili, and it was certainly employing heavy-handed deterrence, particularly with its large military exercise that ended in early August.[46] But on 7 August, Russia had only minimal forces present near the Roki Tunnel leading from

Russia to South Ossetia. Medvedev was on a cruise on the Volga; Putin, now prime minister, was at the Beijing Olympic Games; and the defence minister was on vacation on the Black Sea coast. In short, both sides were preparing for a war, but neither was planning for the war that actually happened.

The war itself should thus be seen as a classic security dilemma, in which escalation spirals spark conflict despite a lack of aggressive intent. That said, tensions between Russia and Georgia had grown that spring and summer in part because of the zero-sum approach of some Western countries, particularly the US under the Bush administration. With the exception of Germany's foreign minister, Frank-Walter Steinmeier, no visible effort was made at preventative diplomacy involving Moscow. Indeed, the Bucharest misadventure did not cause Washington to give up the push for MAP; after the summit, and even after the war, it still pressed its reluctant allies on this point.[47] The Bush administration concluded that 'Russia interpreted the denial of MAP as a green light for action against Georgia'.[48] On that twisted logic, granting MAP would have been a deterrent to future bellicosity. With much of Georgia still smouldering, the idea that now was the time for NATO to antagonise Russia once again found few adherents in Brussels.

Moscow, for its part, could not resist coercing Tbilisi in the run-up to the August war. While it doubtless had to respond to the attack on Tskhinvali, in the event its response was disproportionate and punitive. Not only did the Russian military devastate the Georgian armed forces' capabilities, but it and its South Ossetian confederates expelled more than 25,000 ethnic Georgians from South Ossetia. It might have gained primacy over 20% of Georgia's territory, but it lost the hearts and minds of the rest of the country. By recognising Abkhazia and South Ossetia, Moscow may have avenged the West's move in Kosovo, but it created a range of problems for itself. Russia seemed to have taken the opportunity to implement several objectives once the shooting began, particularly ruling out MAP and NATO membership. In this sense, Georgia suffered more from the Russia–West tug of war than it would have under other circumstances. As Dmitri Trenin of the Carnegie Moscow Center writes, 'For Moscow, the war was not about Georgia as much as about the United States, with Georgia no more than a proxy.'[49]

In the wake of the Georgia war, the West came to view Russia in far more adversarial terms. The US response included cutting off all contact between Pentagon officials and the Russian military; pushing for the suspension of the NATO–Russia relationship; and pulling a civil nuclear agreement from Congress. We now know that a far more drastic response was considered at the highest levels of the Bush administration during the war itself. The president, vice president and other senior officials held a meeting to consider the possibility of using military force to prevent Russia from continuing its military assault on Georgia. Bombardment of the Roki Tunnel that Russian troops used to move into South Ossetia and other 'surgical strikes' were among the options discussed. Upon consideration, the group ruled out any military response.[50] In an interview 18 months later, a Cheney aide said he remained unsure 'whether or not [use of force] should have been more seriously considered'. He went on: 'If Russia continues to assert itself either militarily or through other coercive means to claim a sphere of influence, we will look back at this as a time that they were able to change boundaries in Europe without much reaction. And then we'll say we should have considered harder options.'[51] The US, it was implied, should have gone to war with Russia to rebuff its assertive actions in the region. Without question, the messy equilibrium regarding the regional order that had emerged following the Soviet collapse had been upset.

Enter the EU and the EEU

The European Union, with its institutional hub in Brussels now taking precedence over member-state governments, began to play a more active role in post-Soviet Eurasia after the Georgia war. The French president, Nicolas Sarkozy, then holder of the rotating EU presidency, was the chief negotiator of the cease-fire agreement that helped end the conflict. The EU fielded a monitoring mission in Georgia to keep the peace, which has remained in place ever since. Along with the UN and the OSCE, the EU was appointed a co-chair of the Geneva International Discussions, the negotiating format for Georgia's conflicts.

But the instruments for an enlarged EU role were more geo-ideational and geo-economic than geopolitical. The EU first formalised a policy toward the region in 2004. The European Neighbourhood Policy (ENP) provided a framework for the Union's efforts in its southern and eastern adjacencies with the objective of establishing a stable, prosperous, secure and democratic 'ring of friends'. It set about realising this objective through policy instruments that were 'rule-oriented, non-militarized, and technocratic', claiming the mantle of a 'normative power', not a great power.[52] The ENP strategy paper proposed a straightforward trade to the EU's neighbours: 'In return for concrete progress demonstrating shared values and effective implementation of political, economic, and institutional reforms, including in aligning legislation with the *acquis*, the EU's neighbourhood should benefit from the prospect of closer economic integration with the EU.'[53] This outwardly innocuous approach belied both the emerging zero-sum intentions of some member states and the zero-sum impact of the EU's normative instruments – an exercise par excellence in geo-ideational politics with geo-economic consequences.

Although, as noted above, Russia's regulatory- and trade-policy convergence efforts with Brussels were still more advanced than those of its neighbours in 2005, that balance shifted briskly as its relationship with the EU deteriorated. Solana recalls 'holes' emerging in the Four Common Spaces programme 'very soon' after its adoption, and notes that within two years relations were at an impasse.[54] At the same time, the EU's relations with some of the In-Betweens, particularly Ukraine, grew closer. The 2004 big-bang enlargement, adding ten new member states with 80m citizens, was a factor. Belarus, Moldova and Ukraine (particularly after Romania's EU accession in 2007) now bordered EU members to the west. This subjected them to the 'shadow effect', as Tom Casier calls it, that the EU has on its neighbours: both through the externalisation of internal policies (e.g., product standards imposed on imported goods) and through the 'gravitational pull' of its prosperity and good governance, the EU unintentionally has a bearing on proximate states 'because of its mere existence'.[55] The EU had also just launched the ENP, and was intentionally acting to influence the political economy of its neighbours. As was the case with NATO, the new East Central European members altered the balance within the Union's bureaucracy and political bodies in favour of more interaction with the neighbours and more distance from Russia.

The geo-economic form of EU engagement with the In-Betweens set the stage for a clash with Russia. After the PCAs of the 1990s expired (most had a lifespan of ten years), Brussels settled on Association Agreements (AAs) as the framework for drawing in those states in the region that aspired to integrate with the EU. The AAs feature Deep and Comprehensive Free Trade Area agreements (DCFTAs) at their core. The AA was explicitly an alternative to full EU membership, but it was nonetheless based on the core bargain of the accession process. The EU opens itself to aspirant countries (via visa-free travel, lowered trade barriers, access to internal preferences for everything from education to government procurement) in return for their conformity to the three Copenhagen Criteria (named for the city where they were agreed in 1993): consolidation of democratic institutions and protection of human rights, a market economy, and adoption of the *acquis*, the body of EU laws and regulations. In practice, the emphasis has always been on the third of these.

It should be stressed that fully fledged accession has never been an option for the In-Betweens. But the geo-economic distinction between full membership and the AA/DCFTA model is less ironclad on closer inspection. The AA obliges aspirant countries to change a vast array of standards, regulations and laws to conform with those enshrined in the EU *acquis*. It further prescribes that their future legislation be compatible with the *acquis*; future EU decisions regarding issues covered by the AA must be enforced by the aspirant country. Over time, the AAs would, if implemented, fold these countries into the EU's geo-economic space.

The AA also has shades of geopolitics, even if of the dull, procedure-obsessed EU variety. It creates a ministerial-level Association Council, which gathers regularly and is invested with the power to make decisions regarding AA implementation; a senior-official-level Association Committee; a Parliamentary Association Committee, composed of parliamentarians from the EU and the partner; a Civil Society Platform; and sector-specific committees. All these bodies have equal EU and partner-state representation. In the case of Ukraine, there are also summit meetings at the presidential level.

As Romano Prodi, former president of the European Commission, put it, the AA/DCFTA model provides these countries with 'everything but the institutions', full integration with the Union but no direct participation in the decision-making bodies in Brussels.[56] A country that fully implements the AA would become like Norway, which remains outside the EU but as a member of the European Economic Area (the EU's single market) must comply with the *acquis*. The main practical difference is that Oslo, unlike member-state capitals, cannot take part in EU policymaking.

The requirement to adopt the *acquis* was a powerful lever for reforming the domestic political economies of the new EU members in East Central Europe. So it was perfectly understandable that the EU chose to make this same compendium of rules its primary means of engagement with the In-Betweens, all of which are urgently in need of reform. But the AA does not just spur reform; it is also a geo-economic and geo-ideational exercise. On the macro level, the DCFTA precludes membership of any other customs union (including, as we shall see, the one Russia began ginning up in the same period); put differently, membership of a customs union precludes signing the DCFTA. Classic customs unions oblige members to relinquish national decision-making on tariffs and related matters to a supranational body; the DCFTA by definition requires signatories to maintain such prerogatives for themselves. The inherent take-it-or-leave-it and one-size-fits-all nature of the DCFTA also eliminates the intermediate option many states pursued before: some meshing with both Russia and the EU. It would leave states highly integrated with the EU, while commercial links to Russia (and other CIS countries) would attenuate over time. All 12 non-EU former Soviet republics had, since 1992, shared the same regulatory and technical standards, measurements and certification formats.[57] If one of them were to replace these with (more rigorous) EU standards, its trade with the EU would be facilitated, while trade with other CIS countries could be hindered relative to the status quo ante. And given the nature of the agreement, AA signatories would have to adapt to many EU economic-policy decisions in the future. Brussels would gain pre-eminent influence over policymaking in signatory countries, displacing the influence of any other outside actor. The EU operated on the assumption that its normative hegemony was unassailable.

Russia was anything but welcoming of this new EU activism. But Brussels acted as if Russia did not exist. There were no consultations with Moscow, even though Russian officials had begun to object stridently. The hypersensitivity over steps that could evoke the ghosts of Yalta effectively ruled out conversing with Russia about Ukraine or any other In-Between. In fact, doing so would not have been unprecedented. On the eve of the admission of the Baltics and five other ex-communist countries in 2004, extensive trilateral negotiations had taken place among the EU, Russia and the soon-to-be members. Adjustments were made to accommodate Russian concerns, ranging from an extended adjustment period on aluminium exports to Hungary to special transit arrangements between the exclave of Kaliningrad and the rest of Russia.[58]

Even if Russia had welcomed the EU's involvement with the In-Betweens, the AA/DCFTA model might not have been the right policy instrument for the region. Better formal laws and regulations cannot cure basic pathologies of governance in these countries, which stem from corrupt informal political-economic practices and feeble and often imitative democratic institutions. As we will see, no hard evidence to date has shown that the agreements produced positive changes in governance in the three countries that eventually signed up: Moldova, Georgia and Ukraine.

In May 2009, EU policies toward the six In-Betweens were enhanced and grouped under the banner of the Eastern Partnership. The Commission described it as 'a real step change in relations with our Eastern neighbours, with a significant upgrading of political, economic and trade relations.

The goal is to strengthen the prosperity and stability of these countries, and thus the security of the EU.'[59] Notwithstanding these lofty ambitions, the Eastern Partnership exacerbated the regional contestation. Although some differentiation was to emerge years later, the policy was initially the same for all the In-Betweens – regardless of their level of involvement in Russia-led institutions, or their adherence to the first two Copenhagen Criteria of democracy and market reform. For example, the decision to include Belarus, Russia's closest ally, and arguably the most authoritarian government in the region, created a strong impression that geopolitics was driving EU decision-making.

Russia was not pleased. To Solana, it was apparent almost instantly that the initiative was raising eyebrows, and worse, in Moscow.[60] As Russian Foreign Minister Sergei Lavrov put it in 2009, 'We are accused of having spheres of influence. But what is the Eastern Partnership, if not an attempt to extend the EU's sphere of influence, including to Belarus?'[61] It did not help that prominent European politicians and commentators viewed the programme in precisely these terms. As one German analyst wrote in response to Lavrov's question, 'The answer, of course, is yes. … In the post-Soviet space, neutrality is not an option for Europe. … We must face up to the fact that we are engaged in a systemic competition [with Russia].'[62]

Russia's negative reaction to the EU's foray into the In-Between countries thus was apparent several years before the Ukraine crisis began. So too was the reality that many members of the EU, particularly the new ones, always regarded the Eastern Partnership as an initiative intended to wrest their neighbours from Moscow's grasp. Russia, in turn, rejected EU efforts on principle; if Brussels wanted to proceed, it would have to come to the Kremlin and kiss the ring. As the Russian analyst Andrei Zagorski puts it, 'Moscow specifically underlines that no attempt at regional cooperation in this part of Europe is possible if it does not involve the Russian Federation.'[63] Russia's dogged pursuit of a say in other countries' decisions made the EU more determined to proceed with its plans and less inclined to discuss them with Moscow. As German Chancellor Angela Merkel told parliament in November 2013, 'To put it unequivocally – the countries must decide themselves on their future direction. Third parties cannot have the right of veto.'[64] The regional elites had incentives to stoke this competition since they knew that their clout would be maximised if multiple external patrons were in competition with one another.

Less than a month after the Eastern Partnership was launched, Russia countered with its own initiative, and Moscow-led integration in post-Soviet Eurasia finally gained traction after almost 20 years of dithering. In June 2009, Russia, Kazakhstan and Belarus agreed to form an institutionalised Customs Union effective from 1 January 2010.[65] While any number of past geo-economic efforts had been stillborn, this for once was a concrete step. The failure of previous initiatives had led Moscow to trim down its ambitions for membership of the Customs Union, starting with only the two states most willing to move forward.

In form, the Customs Union was a significant departure from past post-Soviet practices and was closer to the early stages of the EU than to the moribund CIS. Under the 2009 agreement, a Customs Union Commission was to function as a permanent decision-making and adjudicative mechanism; it, and not the national governments, had the authority to set tariffs. The three founders quickly moved to create something more substantial, progressing from the creation of a single market in 2012 to the Eurasian Economic Union (EEU) in 2015. With the forming of the EEU, a Eurasian Economic Commission (EEC), a fully fledged institution with its own bureaucracy, replaced the Customs Union Commission and a court was created to resolve trade disputes.

In its initial stages, this project should be graded as a guarded success.[66] Customs posts were removed on the borders between Russia and the two other members. EEC data shows a large increase in intra-Customs Union trade in 2010–12. Once Russia became a member of the World Trade Organization (WTO) in 2012, the Customs Union had to adopt a system of rules in line with WTO standards, hence exporting international norms to other members that did not belong to the WTO (Kazakhstan joined in 2015). Decision-making is conducted by consensus at the level of Council of the EEC, a body comprising deputy prime ministers from all member states with a rotating presidency. While there is evidence of Russia's using political, economic and security instruments to keep other members in line, the need to achieve unanimous votes on major decisions has at times forced it to compromise. This requirement also gave the smaller member states a voice on policy decisions that were previously Russia's exclusive prerogative. EEU officials professed an aspiration to emulate the best practices of the EU.

The EEU began as a technocratic, if geo-economic, endeavour, even though some outsiders have had doubts about the economic logic behind it. Be that as it may, Russia's great-power aspirations and the intensifying zero-sum dynamic in the region between it and the EU soon began to shape Eurasian economic integration and to link it to geopolitics. In an article in the daily *Izvestiya* written in October 2011, as he was beginning his campaign to return to the presidency, then-prime minister Putin laid out his vision for the future of the bloc. He envisioned a 'model of a powerful supranational association, capable of becoming one of the poles of the modern world and of playing the role of an effective inter-linkage between Europe and the dynamic Asia-Pacific region'.[67] What was then just a customs union – focused on mundane work like tariff unification and food-safety standards – had been given the geopolitical mission of ensuring Russia's international heft for the twenty-first century. In the article, Putin called this future entity the 'Eurasian Union'.

He had not cleared the rebranding with Nursultan Nazarbaev, the president of Kazakhstan, who was incensed, and demanded that 'Economic' be inserted into the name. The tiff with Putin was about far more than just word choice. Neither Nazarbaev nor Belarusian President Alexander Lukashenko was interested in more than economics, and they were particularly skittish about any effort to impinge on their political independence. Furthermore, they had not signed up for Moscow's omnibus geopolitical vision for the EEU.[68] A few weeks after Putin published his article, Nazarbaev wrote his own piece for *Izvestiya*, in which he stressed that 'economic interests, and not abstract geopolitical ideas and slogans, are the main driver of the integration process'.[69] That he was victorious on the name issue demonstrates that the EEU does give the non-Russian members some influence over important decisions.

In his *Izvestiya* article, Putin had noted that while 'we welcome other CIS partners' joining [the Union] … we do not plan to rush or compel anyone [to do so]'. He claimed that joining the Union need not contradict others' 'European choice', because in the future, there would be bloc-to-bloc rapprochement talks. 'So joining the Eurasian Union … will allow each of its members to integrate with Europe faster and on more advantageous terms.'[70] Unlike Putin's 2005 comments in Kyiv, when he said that the approximation of Russian and EU legislation would allow its neighbours to integrate with both simultaneously, he now envisioned two separate blocs in Europe that would cut deals with one another but remain distinct. Under these circumstances, bandwagoning with Russia would be the only sensible option for CIS countries. The unspoken message to the In-Betweens was clear: Moscow wants to determine the extent and pace of their integration with the EU. Dealing directly with Brussels was not advisable.

The geo-economic dimension of the regional contestation had now taken on more significance, with both sides pursuing zero-sum policies. Russia, reverting to its coercive instincts, put pressure on the four In-Betweens that were flirting with the EU to block their Association Agreements and in some cases also to join the EEU. In the Georgian case, Moscow's pull was limited; diplomatic ties had been severed in 2008 and Russia was no longer Georgia's main trading partner. Moscow threatened to raise tariffs if Tbilisi signed the AA, but never followed through. In this case, the threat failed to sway Tbilisi; its AA was inked in June 2014.

Moscow did resort to economic coercion with Moldova. In September 2013, two months before Chisinau planned to initial its AA, Moldovan wine exports to Russia were banned on public-health grounds. Further sanitary restrictions were imposed in April and July 2014 and the next month Russia suspended tariff-free imports for 19 categories of goods.[71] Russia's economic bullying failed to affect Moldova's choice to proceed with the AA, which it signed at the same time as Georgia in June 2014.

Russia also turned the screws on Armenia, and here it worked. Armenia had been negotiating an AA with the EU for three years, and the two sides planned to initial the document in November 2013. However, in September 2013 Armenian President Serzh Sargsyan abruptly changed course and announced his country's intention to drop the AA and join the EEU. He was widely reported to have been put under significant pressure from Moscow to do so.

Armenia's about-face reflected its deep dependence on Russia not only for economic prosperity but also for security. Russian state firms own most of its utilities, including the railway and the natural-gas distributor, while private finan-cial-industrial groups from Russia dominate other strategic sectors. And, given Armenia's economic isolation – its borders with hostile Azerbaijan and Turkey have been closed off for 20 years – and resulting poverty, Yerevan has no alternative to Moscow's patronage. It also relies on Russian security guar-antees and military assistance in its conflict with Azerbaijan over Nagorno-Karabakh. After a year of talks that led to a number of concessions, including on import duties and gas prices, Armenia signed the EEU treaty in October 2014, becoming a rare case of a trade-bloc participant that shares no borders with its fellow members. Talks on membership for Kyrgyzstan, which shares borders with Kazakhstan (and China) but not with Russia, also began in 2014, and Bishkek joined in August 2015.

A deceptive calm

Although the geo-economic zero-sum interplay between Russia and the EU picked up after the 2008 war, in the period between that conflict and the Ukraine crisis in 2014 there was a noticeable diminution of the intensity of the overall regional contestation. However, this intermission arose from contingent, circumstantial factors that served to paper over the underlying problem without a serious effort to negate its causes.

The first factor preceded the short war in the South Caucasus by three months: the swearing in of Dmitry Medvedev as Russian president. While the differences between him and Putin should not be exaggerated, his presidency did have a positive effect on the relationship with the West. Most importantly, he wasn't Putin, who had come to be personally associated with a truculent approach to foreign policy. Medvedev was a fresh face without the same political baggage. He also did not share the same sense of personal betrayal that Putin seemed to wear on his sleeve in dealings with Western leaders. Additionally, his agenda of economic modernisation led him to seek some measure of normalisation in relations with the West.[72]

Soon after the changing of the guard in Moscow, leadership turned over in Washington. Barack Obama, and his team that took office in January 2009, were not interested in playing 'great games' (a reference to the nineteenth-century rivalry between Britain and Russia in Central Asia) or pursuing other policies that were egregiously confrontational toward Russia in post-Soviet Eurasia. 'Reject idea of "Great Game" in Central Asia' was a bullet point on an official presentation of the administration's Russia policy.[73] The US ceased pushing the NATO MAP issue for Georgia and Ukraine, and generally dialled back the competitive dynamic in the region.

A third leadership change also contributed to the lull: the election of Viktor Yanukovych as president of Ukraine in February 2010. Yanukovych never fully deserved the moniker 'pro-Russian', but certainly he was far less gratuitously anti-Russian than his predecessor Yushchenko. Soon after taking office, Yanukovych signed a new foreign-policy doctrine renouncing Ukraine's NATO membership aspirations in favour of *pozablokovist'* ('non-blocness', i.e., neutrality). In April 2010, he signed a 25-year extension of Russia's lease on the Black Sea Fleet in return for a discounted gas price. Ukraine, always the most important arena of competition, had removed itself from the geopolitical game (though not the geo-economic one, as we shall see).

All three leadership changes facilitated the 'reset' in US–Russia relations and the improvement in Russia–Europe relations in 2009–12. There was some positive spillover into

West–Russia interaction in post-Soviet Eurasia. The US facility at Kyrgyzstan's Manas airport, a stopping point for US soldiers and materiel on the way to Afghanistan, was a good example. In February 2009, Russia offered US$2 billion in assistance to Bakiev, Kyrgyzstan's strongman, in return for evicting the US from Manas. Toward the end of its time in office, the Bush administration had treated the basing arrangements as an exclusively bilateral issue with the Kyrgyzstanis, which had led Moscow to conclude that the US intended to stay there indeterminately and/or to use Manas as part of a strategy to encircle Russia. Rather than trying to outbid Moscow, the Obama administration sought Russian buy-in. As Michael McFaul, architect of the reset who served as senior director for Russia on the National Security Council staff from Obama's inauguration until he became ambassador to Moscow in November 2011, recalled, Obama used his first meeting with Medvedev to make clear that he did not care to engage in zero-sum rivalry in the region: 'He said, "Help me understand[,] President Medvedev[,] why you want us to leave Manas. [B]ecause what are our soldiers doing? They are flying into Afghanistan after a short amount of time in Kyrgyzstan and they are fighting people that if we weren't fighting them you would have to be fighting them."'[74] Medvedev responded positively, and not only stopped attempts to dislodge the US from Manas but agreed to shipments across Russia by rail for materiel needed by American forces in Afghanistan and even to military overflights for getting troops to the theatre. This route via Russia to Afghanistan would prove indispensable when Pakistan barred the US from using the Khyber Pass following the raid that killed Osama bin Laden.

When Kyrgyzstan descended into anarchy after Bakiev was ousted by angry crowds in April 2010, most observers assumed that Moscow had orchestrated the unrest as revenge for Bakiev reneging on a promise to shut down the base. But instead of indulging in zero-sum games as usual, Russia and the US worked in concert, pursuing back-channel talks that facilitated Bakiev's safe escape into exile in Belarus. Consultations between Moscow and Washington not only prevented conflict between them – in the one country where both had military outposts – but also led to the coordination of humanitarian assistance. Obama and Medvedev went so far as to issue a joint statement on Kyrgyzstan in June 2010.[75] Kyrgyzstan was an easy case – it is small, remote and impoverished, a non-candidate for NATO or EU integration – but US–Russia comity following political unrest in the region was extraordinary nonetheless.

The EU and Russia had their own reset of sorts in this period, leading to a new framework called the Partnership for Modernization in 2010. Even the NATO–Russia Council came to life, with collaboration on concrete issues ranging from Afghanistan to theatre missile defence. Medvedev attended the Lisbon NATO summit in November 2010 to hold a leader-level meeting of the Council. The 29 heads of state and government issued a statement that 'we have embarked on a new stage of cooperation towards a true strategic partnership'.[76] The atmospherics of Russia's relations with the West were significantly better than they had been in the wake of the 2008 war. As Vyacheslav Nikonov, a hawkish foreign-policy analyst and government adviser, said, 'The overall climate is better than it has been since the time of perestroika.'[77]

But the fundamental conflict relating to the region had not been addressed and therefore remained a landmine that could detonate at any time if activated. As one of us wrote at the time, 'the current pause in unconstructive US–Russia rivalry in post-Soviet Eurasia is highly contingent and unlikely to be sustained by inertia'.[78] Even during this more relaxed period, no tangible progress was made on dealing with the problem at its roots.

Russia did try to begin a conversation on the subject. Speaking in Berlin in June 2008, Medvedev proposed negotiations on a new European security treaty. He elaborated on what its general contents might be in a speech in France in October 2008, after the August war:

> The events in the Caucasus have only confirmed how absolutely right the concept of a new European security treaty is today. It would give us every possibility of building an integrated and solid system of comprehensive security. This system should be equal for all states – without isolating anyone and without zones with different levels of security. It should consolidate the Euro-Atlantic region as a whole on the basis of uniform rules of the game.[79]

Harking back to Gorbachev's 'common European home', he emphasised the concept of 'indivisibility of security' that was a cornerstone of the 1990 Charter of Paris.

At the same time, Medvedev was also articulating a starkly divergent foreign-policy priority. Moscow, he said, had demarcated its neighbourhood as 'a traditional sphere of Russian interests'.[80] 'For Russia, as for other countries, there are regions in which it has privileged interests.'[81] The geo-idea was clear: Russia has a natural right to pre-eminence in its proximate environs. The problem is that if Russia has a sphere, the countries in it have to be insecure (or spoken for) in order for Russia to be secure, which would suggest that security is divisible after all. Medvedev's use of the phrase, particularly after the war with Georgia, set off sirens in the region and the West. US Vice President Joe Biden felt the need to rebut it in his speech that launched the US–Russia reset: 'We will not recognize any nation having a sphere of influence.'[82]

After Western partners demanded specifics regarding Medvedev's proposal, Russia published a draft treaty in November 2009.[83] The document, while grounded in widely accepted principles like respect for territorial integrity and political independence, and the renunciation of the use of force, was deeply flawed. It was a legally binding treaty, the most weighty of all international agreements, which tend to come after a build-up of less formal arrangements that help generate support among domestic constituencies needed for ratification. It tackled core disagreements by creating new bureaucracies and crisis-response mechanisms. It also included provisions that would have obliged all states and existing organisations (including the EU and NATO) to ensure that their decisions 'do not affect significantly the security of any Party or Parties to the Treaty'. Given the state of relations among countries in the region, the draft was dead on arrival.

The text was also a distraction from the opening that Medvedev's initiative could have been: to begin much-needed dialogue on the regional order. Western governments focused on the objectionable elements in the text and declined the call for high-level talks. In a speech in Paris in early 2010, the secretary of state, Hillary Clinton, delivered the official US response: 'common goals are best pursued in the context of existing institutions, such as the OSCE and the NATO–Russia Council, rather than by negotiating new treaties, as Russia has suggested'.[84] To put it in plain language, the regional order did not need any rethinking. The West was unwilling even to begin a conversation on the subject. The only dialogue to take place was at the working level in the OSCE – named the 'Corfu Process' for the Greek island where it began – that led nowhere.

Warning signs cropped up repeatedly. When meeting Russian counterparts in late 2009, a senior US official 'emphasized that Russia's efforts to assert a regional sphere of influence posed a threat to the reset in bilateral relations'.[85] In the same period, the US opposed any dealings between NATO and the CSTO, out of the conviction that 'validation of the CSTO could further strengthen Moscow's influence over our Central Asian [partners]'.[86] In June 2010, a German–Russian initiative to move forward on resolving the Transnistria frozen conflict while creating a new consultation mechanism between Russia and the EU on regional security not only failed to deliver on both counts, but also generated accusations that Berlin had offered Moscow a veto over EU decision-making.[87]

Even when interests overlapped, Russia and the West often failed to cooperate. In the months before the December 2010 re-election of Belarusian President Lukashenko, the US and the EU offered Minsk incentives to conduct a free and fair vote, and threatened further sanctions if not. Moscow sent strong signals that it had lost patience with Lukashenko (for backtracking on economic integration, among other gripes) and threatened not to recognise the results of the poll. But neither the West nor Russia made an effort to consult about Belarus or in any way to coordinate their efforts. The Kremlin seems to have grown apprehensive that the only alternative to the incumbent was the ostensibly pro-Western opposition candidate, and decided to throw its support behind Lukashenko in the final days before the poll. The result – an election of dubious legitimacy that was marred by violence against unarmed protesters during unrest that followed the vote – served no one's interests but his. In short, even at a time of unusually calm Russia–West ties, the zero-sum dynamic in post-Soviet Eurasia persisted, albeit at a lower pitch.

In late 2011 and 2012, the fleeting reset of the broader relationship came to an end. The US and Russia were divided by a string of bitter disputes over crises in other regions, particularly in Libya and Syria. Putin's return to the Kremlin and the protests in Moscow and other cities in late 2011 and 2012 further poisoned the well. In 2013 Russia sheltered the former American intelligence contractor, Edward Snowden, who had leaked thousands of secret documents, compounding mistrust. EU–Russia relations also soured as the regional geo-economic tussle intensified. By the time the Ukraine crisis hit, the climate was far less conducive to handling a contingency without severe conflict than it had been at the height of the reset.

CHAPTER THREE

Breaking point

With all the fundamental disputes lurking just beneath the surface, the period of deceptive calm in the regional contestation could not last long. It came to an end in spectacular fashion in Ukraine, by far the largest and most strategically significant of the In-Betweens. Enmity over Ukraine set the stage for a crisis that drew in the great powers and transformed relations among them.

Ukraine is more populous than the other five In-Betweens taken together, second only to Russia among the former Soviet republics. The word Ukraine literally means 'borderland', and that is what it had again become by this time: surrounded by members of EU and NATO to the west and the EEU and CSTO to the north and east. The relatively Russia-friendly Viktor Yanukovych had replaced the Western-leaning Viktor Yushchenko as president in 2010, and shored up frayed ties with Moscow. But Yanukovych was not eager to throw his country unqualifiedly into Russia's embrace, preferring to walk a tightrope between it and the West and collect as much rent as possible in the process. The rub was that both external patrons were now seeking irreconcilable commitments from him.

Raising the stakes

The election of Yanukovych muted geopolitical competition regarding Ukraine, particularly as it concerned NATO membership. But his early concessions to Moscow – the commitment to non-bloc status and the lease extension for the Russian Black Sea Fleet base – did not satisfy the Kremlin. It became clear in the first year of his presidency that Russia was going to advance on another front, geo-economics, seeking much greater sway over Ukraine than Yanukovych was prepared to give.

Despite the sizeable discount on gas Yanukovych obtained from the 2010 Black Sea Fleet deal, Ukraine was still paying more for gas than it could afford. After another contract dispute in the winter of 2008–09 that ended in a cut-off and Ukraine once again diverting supplies meant for Europe, Russia, unlike in 2006, had held firm for two weeks in the middle of a frigid winter. There was significant collateral damage – several East Central European countries had difficulty heating and powering their cities – but when the dust settled Kyiv had signed the first contract free of subsidised pricing, which by that point had cost Russia more than US$16bn.[1] The trouble was that Ukraine would need an overhaul of its energy-intensive industries and wasteful public utilities to be able to afford the price in that 2009 contract (even with the fleet-deal discount, Kyiv was paying double the 2008 cost in 2010).

Since such politically risky market reforms were not Yanukovych's cup of tea, Moscow had leverage over the new president and was prepared to use it. Just weeks after the Black Sea Fleet deal, the Kremlin was said to have put on the table a proposal for Gazprom to acquire Naftohaz, Ukraine's state-owned gas monopoly, in return for another discount.[2] Naftohaz is a cash cow for plugging holes in the government budget and lining the pockets of insiders. It has also been the tie that binds the EU to Ukraine, since it manages the transit of Russian gas heading across Ukraine to Europe. Yanukovych was not about to give that away. He did, though, sign early cooperation agreements with Moscow in the steel, chemical, shipbuilding, aviation and nuclear-power sectors. The Russians were pushing him very hard; Medvedev met him seven times in the first 100 days of his term. After the seventh meeting, an exhausted Yanukovych said, 'we can't go on like this'. Medvedev shot back, 'maybe we can't, but we must'.[3]

Most significant geo-economically, Moscow importuned Ukraine under its new leadership to become a member of the nascent Customs Union. Then-prime minister Putin did not mince words on this score during his first meeting with Yanukovych, issuing a public entreaty for Ukraine to 'join the Customs Union'.[4] The Russian demand significantly upped the ante, as the Customs Union was much more far-reaching and binding than any of the previous Russia-led regional endeavours, most recently the SES. Partly this was about timing: the Customs Union got up and running the month of Yanukovych's election. But Russia's impatience seemed to be driven more by the growing geo-economic contest with the EU in the region. The Eastern Partnership had just been unveiled, and Ukraine had by now negotiated much of the text for an AA and the DCFTA within it. Locking in Ukraine's Customs Union membership would have boosted Russia's pet project and blocked Ukraine from proceeding with the EU deal. Moscow was not interested in allowing the Ukrainians to have their cake and eat it. The Kremlin meant to thwart the EU's geo-economic expansion by expanding its own geo-economic sphere. Hence the Customs Union offer was presented as a binary choice – in or out – unlike prior initiatives that gave Ukraine a menu of options.

When Yanukovych rejected the offer, Moscow put forth tantalising carrots – a further discount on gas prices, and tariff benefits for key industries – at a time when the Ukrainian economy was still reeling from the 2008 economic crisis and the gas-price hike stemming from the 2009 contract.[5] Russian officials also frequently cited studies showing major economic benefits for Ukraine from Customs Union membership, and made claims that the DCFTA would cause it grievous economic harm.[6] In April 2011, Yanukovych tried to meet Moscow halfway, proposing a '3+1' formula for the relationship.[7] Russia rejected the idea out of hand. As the head of the Customs Union Commission, Sergei Glaziev, said, 'Outside of the Customs Union it will be impossible to make progress. … The only option for Ukraine is full participation in the work of the Customs Union. All other formulas have no basis to them.'[8] Kyiv was to halt its talks with Brussels in favour of immersion in Russia's most ambitious geo-economic initiative since the collapse of the Soviet Union.

The Ukrainian leadership was unmoved. It initialled the AA in March 2012, leaving only technical and legal formalities before the signing ceremony. But on a political level, Ukraine's relationship with the EU had begun to sour. A particular irritant was the sentencing of Tymoshenko, the former prime minister and Yanukovych's arch-foe, to a seven-year prison term, on trumped-up charges. As EU rebukes for this blatant abuse of power grew vociferous, Ukraine seemed to waver in its preference for the AA over Customs Union membership. 'Today', the Ukrainian ambassador to Moscow said in November 2012, 'we don't say either yes or no [to Customs Union membership]'. But, he added, if Ukraine's trade with the bloc grows, and the EU's economic woes deepen, 'the answer will more likely be yes than no'.[9]

Yanukovych's government was divided on the issue. The president seemed to be mindful that the treatment of Tymoshenko had become a litmus test for the EU, and wanted to buttress his bargaining position with Brussels by demonstrating that he had other options, in keeping with the Ukrainian tradition of playing one party off the other. Some lesser officials, often those linked to industries that exported mostly to the EU, ruled out Customs Union membership, while others suggested it could be possible in the future.[10] Ukraine's economic circumstances were on a downward slide, and Yanukovych and his ministers still coveted an extra gas discount from Russia to relieve the pain.

More important than these tactical considerations, Yanukovych's waffling reflected the bedrock economic realities of his country. Ukraine's trade was divided almost evenly between the EU and Russia. So Yanukovych's attempt to avoid a binary choice between them was understandable, even if other motives were also in play. Unfortunately, neither the EU nor Russia offered him a way to do so. Speaking for the EU in December 2012, one official pronounced it 'impossible for Ukraine to align with both [the EU and the Customs Union] at the same time. Ukraine should choose which path to take. … Even partial accession to the Customs Union … would be problematic.'[11] The next month, a senior Russian diplomat used more colourful language to make the same point from Moscow's angle: 'Ukraine wants to simultaneously maintain two vectors: both to join the EU [sic] … and to participate in the Customs Union, but only in those areas where it stands to gain. But things don't work that way. You cannot be a little bit pregnant.'[12] A geo-economic confrontation was in the offing. Both the EU and Russia were less interested in preventing it than in prevailing in it.

Russia seemed to soften its position in May 2013, when Ukraine, while in the last stages of negotiations with the EU on the AA, signed a memorandum on cooperation with the EEC, granting Kyiv observer status. Yanukovych called European Commission president José Manuel Barroso the same day to reassure him that the memorandum did not contradict the AA. But Russia was not content with Yanukovych's plan to integrate only to the extent that Ukraine's EU commitments allowed. The very day the memorandum was signed, Glaziev said 'Observer status is only granted to states that want to join our integration project. … Since we agreed to give Ukraine observer status … that means Ukraine intends to join our union.'[13] Ukraine had never spoken of such an intention.

Moscow was still pushing hard on Yanukovych – but its bottom line seemed to have shifted. Some observers claimed that Russia would still accept nothing less than full Ukrainian membership of the Customs Union (and subsequently the EEU). Certainly that was Moscow's preferred outcome, but by 2013 it was no longer issuing ultimatums to Ukraine to join straight away. The heavy-handed pressure that began that summer came in the context of the impending signing of the AA, planned for the November summit of the EU and the In-Betweens (in EU-speak, the Eastern Partnership countries) in Vilnius. And if that went ahead, Ukraine would be forever lost for Russia-led integration efforts. Russia was now primarily concerned with forestalling that outcome and keeping the prospect of eventual integration open, rather than demanding immediate Ukrainian membership.

The instrument Moscow deployed was characteristically blunt. Beginning in July 2013, Russia imposed trade sanctions on Ukraine, first by cutting off imports of confectionery products, fruit, vegetables and poultry. It then hit steel manufacturers and other exporters with cumbersome new customs procedures. 'De facto, there is a complete halt on Ukrainian exports', the Ukrainian manufacturers trade group reported.[14] For several days the next month, the Russian authorities applied extensive customs checks to all Ukrainian imports, all but totally blocking them.

Although normal trade resumed in less than a week, the message of these actions was clear: if Kyiv were to proceed with the AA, it should expect a disruption in bilateral trade with Russia.[15] Specifically, Moscow threatened to scrap Ukraine's trade preferences under the CIS's extant free-trade pact, an effective increase in average tariffs of more than ten percentage points. It was estimated that this would have reduced Ukrainian exports to Russia by 17% per year, shaving off 1.7% of Ukraine's GDP annually.[16] Russian spokesmen used a spurious economic argument to justify this threat as something other than crude coercion: they claimed that European goods would enter Ukraine duty free under the DCFTA, and then 'flood' the Russian market by exploiting CIS free-trade rules governing Russia–Ukraine commerce. As Putin said, 'We say, it's your choice … but keep in mind that we will be forced to defend our market.'[17] Perhaps such a risk existed on the margins, but rules of origin – the globally accepted benchmarks for determining the national source of a product – would have allowed the Russian customs authorities to distinguish between EU and Ukrainian goods in the vast majority of cases. Why repeatedly make an argument that most trade experts considered facetious? A charitable explanation is that many in Moscow made worst-case assumptions about the AA and DCFTA due to the lack of dialogue with Ukraine and the EU on the subject. Or, more likely, this talking point could have been a cover story for Moscow's efforts to block the AA, which would certainly have redirected Ukraine's trade away from Russia in the long term.

The Russian squeeze on Ukraine's economy did not stop Yanukovych from pushing ahead with the AA; his government formally approved the final draft on 18 September. But furious wheeling and dealing was ongoing away from public view. Yanukovych knew that the EU was keen to have the AA signed at the November Vilnius summit and angled for concessions from Brussels in the final weeks. Despite voluminous evidence that Ukraine's politics were becoming more authoritarian and its political economy increasingly monopolised by Yanukovych's family and inner circle, the EU was still ready to sign the AA with Kyiv if it allowed Tymoshenko to leave prison for medical treatment in Germany.

The EU's focus on the Tymoshenko case had blown its significance out of proportion. Her imprisonment after a politically motivated prosecution was just one example of broader failings in Ukrainian democratic governance that had become more acute under Yanukovych but long predated him. A weak judicial system was chronically subject to manipulation by patrons in the executive branch and the business elite. But Brussels' need to emerge victorious in what was now an open geo-economic bidding war with Moscow trumped the principle that greater integration should only be offered in return for reform. The conditionality for signing the AA was thus reduced to a single symbolically rich but systemically insignificant step.

Brussels even dropped that residual demand in the end. In the weeks before the Vilnius summit, Yanukovych seized on the EU's visible eagerness to move ahead, with the apparent expectation not only that Brussels would give up on Tymoshenko, but that it would also provide financial compensation to offset the cost of Moscow's expected retaliation, which he claimed would amount to US$160bn. While the EU declined to pay the financial ransom, it relented on Tymoshenko. Poland had pushed for the concession, arguing that if Ukraine did not sign the AA, it was just a matter of time before Moscow re-established control over the country. 'Never again do we want to have a common border with Russia', the Polish president is said to have informed Chancellor Merkel.[18]

But that was not enough for Yanukovych. Despite the EU's last-minute concession on Tymoshenko, the Ukrainian cabinet issued an order suspending preparations to sign the AA just a week before Vilnius. The same order called for the establishment of a trilateral commission with Russia and the EU to discuss trade relations and the renewal of active dialogue with the countries of the Customs Union on trade and economic issues. While Yanukovych did not stop proclaiming his commitment to European integration, it was clear that the AA would not be signed at Vilnius.

The EU refused to back down. Barroso and the president of the European Council, Herman Van Rompuy, brought two copies of the AA to Vilnius in a last-ditch attempt to seal the deal in person with Yanukovych.[19] When even that could not deliver Yanukovych's signature, European leaders publicly browbeat him during the evening reception, with the cameras rolling. These awkward moves created the distinct impression that motives other than reform and integration were driving EU policy. Washington, having observed the AA negotiations from the sidelines, was in no position to prevent this train wreck.

A few weeks after the meltdown at Vilnius, Putin received Yanukovych in Moscow to celebrate his apparent triumph over the EU. It was an enormously expensive victory: Russia promised to purchase US$15bn in Ukrainian eurobonds and to cut the gas price for Ukraine by more than US$130 per thousand cubic metres, or roughly one-third. At a press conference following the meeting, Putin said, 'To reassure everyone: we did not discuss the issue of Ukraine joining the Customs Union.'[20] Having pushed for full Ukrainian membership of the Customs Union several years earlier, Russia now was prepared to pay a high price just to block the EU agreement and keep the door open for the future.

Yanukovych's calculus remains murky. Perhaps he never intended to sign the AA and simply wanted to garner as many concessions as possible from Russia.[21] A less cynical take is that he did want to go ahead with the AA – until Moscow made it clear that there would be a price to pay for doing so and the EU refused to pick up the tab. Despite the crudeness of Yanukovych's horse-trading, his predicament was ultimately a product of zero-sum jousting between Russia and the EU, which led them to pose a binary choice to his country. Kyiv made plain that it did not want to choose, but was ignored. Even its public call for trilateral talks went unanswered until much later.

Russia's victory was short-lived. Yanukovych returned from Moscow to find a large crowd occupying Kyiv's central Maidan nezalezhnosti (Independence Square), the epicentre of the Orange Revolution in 2004. A group first gathered there in the days following Vilnius to protest Yanukovych's about-face on the AA. But neither that agreement, a highly technical, 2,100-page document that mostly covers distinctly uninspiring subjects such as fishery regulations, nor even a desire to join the EU (supported by only 37% of the population at the time), would have produced the crowds that subsequently emerged.[22] Had Yanukovych allowed those small, peaceful demonstrations to run their course, they would probably have petered out and the protesters returned home. However, his interior ministry moved to disperse the crowd forcefully; the riot police were particularly hard on students camped out on the square. The scenes of brutality inspired more than 500,000 people to take to the streets the next day. Despite the multitude of EU flags on display, the focus of the protests was now on ousting Yanukovych.

In the subsequent weeks, the government and a far-right nationalist vanguard among the protesters, who, unlike the peaceful majority of the diverse crowd, had taken up fire-arms, Molotov cocktails and improvised weapons, escalated the violence. As pandemonium unfolded in Kyiv, Russia and the West, reverting to type, sought to influence events to gain advantage in their contest over Ukraine, with both geo-economics and geopolitics now in play. The Kremlin pushed Yanukovych to crack down harder on the protesters. Its hand could be detected in a packet of repressive laws he rammed through parliament in mid-January, many of them modelled on analogous Russian legislation.

US and EU leaders and diplomats met with and called Yanukovych and his senior ministers dozens of times to urge them to compromise with the Western-leaning opposition and avoid mayhem on the Maidan. US officials were deeply involved in trying to forge a settlement to the crisis; a leaked recording of a conversation between two of them exposed an effort to pick which opposition politicians would sit in a new government. The officials tried to seal the deal, which in the end fell through, before Russia had time to react.[23] Given that the recording was, in all likelihood, made and leaked by Russian operatives, it is safe to assume that the Kremlin believed the US was mounting another regime-change operation, that is, regional geopolitics as usual. Brussels tried to take advantage of the pro-EU leanings of the protesters, mounting a rearguard action to give Yanukovych another chance to sign the AA (on the premise that doing so would satisfy the crowds), and this time dangling the financial assistance it had denied him two months earlier.[24]

Another settlement-that-wasn't

After a particularly gory series of clashes between protesters and police that left dozens dead in mid-February 2014, the Ukrainians and the outside powers took a step back from the abyss. Talks between Yanukovych and the nominal leaders of the Maidan protest movement – it would become clear later that they were not in fact leading the crowds, but being led by them – began in earnest. During three days of negotiations, Yanukovych and three opposition leaders – Oleh Tyahnybok, Vitaliy Klichko and Arseniy Yatsenyuk – hammered out an agreement mediated by the French, Polish and German foreign ministers and a Russian presidential representative. Signed on 21 February, the pact stated that the 2004 amendments to the constitution, which placed limits on the president's powers and had been revoked in 2010, would be restored within 48 hours; a national unity government would be formed within ten days; all illegal weapons were to be surrendered; presidential elections would be held under reformed electoral laws no later than December 2014; and the occupations of streets and buildings would end.[25] Participants reported that Putin called Yanukovych during the talks to urge him to agree to the deal.[26] In what looked like a Russia–West truce, Putin and US President Obama spoke on the phone that night and agreed on the need to implement the arrangement in full and without delay.[27] On paper, the 21 February agreement had elements of a 'pacted' transition, a form of political transformation that is generally more peaceful and democratic than forcing incumbents out of office. It also had the benefit of endorsement by the external powers that had spent much of the previous six months locked in a tug of war over Ukraine.

However, the agreement collapsed immediately, largely due to domestic factors, and became another settlement-that-wasn't. Within hours of the signing, Yanukovych's authority buckled, as police deserted their posts throughout the capital. Protesters freely entered government buildings that riot police had secured hours earlier. Yanukovych fled Kyiv the next day and parliament voted 328–0 to remove him from office – an extra-constitutional act since there had been no statutory impeachment process – and to call new elections. Several days later, he surfaced in Russia.

The Maidan Revolution upended the balance of power among the macroregions of Ukraine. Of Yanukovych's ministers, 75% hailed from the southern and eastern *oblasts* (provinces); in the new government, 60% came from the four westernmost oblasts (where only 12% of Ukraine's population resides) and only two ministers were from the south and east.[28] The speaker of the Verkhovna Rada (the parliament), a prominent Yanukovych ally, quit, and Oleksandr Turchynov, an MP known for his hard-line nationalist positions (and an associate of Tymoshenko, who was released from prison on 21 February), was selected to replace him. As speaker, he by law became acting head of state until a new president was elected. Within days, the Rada confirmed a government headed by Yatsenyuk, a Western-oriented politician; the other ministerial portfolios were divvied up among his party, Tyahnybok's far-right Svoboda party and representatives of the Maidan protesters. The first steps of the post-revolutionary Rada merely reinforced the impression that southern and eastern Ukraine (with their sizeable Russian-speaking minorities), and not just Yanukovych, had been pushed out of power. Two days after Yanukovych's fall, the Rada unwisely voted to repeal a 2012 law that allowed oblasts under certain conditions to use Russian or any other of Ukraine's minority languages for official business, in addition to Ukrainian. Although Turchynov did not sign the repeal in the end, its passage alienated a substantial portion of the population.

Western leaders neither voiced concerns about these developments nor sought a new accord to replace the 21 February agreement, some provisions of which had now been overtaken by events. The day after the change in power, the US declared its 'strong support' for the new authorities.[29] The EU foreign-policy chief, Catherine Ashton, travelled to Kyiv and stated that 'the situation has moved on' and therefore the 21

February pact could be disregarded.[30] Behind the scenes, some Western officials were celebrating the change in government in Kyiv, and saw no need to deal Moscow in, as they had on 21 February when Yanukovych was still in power. The then-US ambassador to Russia, Michael McFaul, later said he received numerous 'high-five emails' from colleagues in the days after the revolution.[31]

The cause for jubilation in Western capitals was their seeming come-from-behind victory in the contest with Russia over Ukraine. The new government was bent on reversing Yanukovych's relatively Russia-friendly foreign policy and resurrecting the EU AA. The elements of the 21 February pact that remained relevant, particularly the formation of a national unity government, the clearing out of protesters from occupied buildings and the confiscation of unregistered firearms, fell by the wayside. Moreover, no high-level outreach with Russia was attempted in the critical days following Yanukovych's fall; Obama did not call Putin again until 1 March. After the interlude of cooperation on 21 February, the zero-sum dynamic was once again ascendant.

Unlike in the West, there were no high fives in the corridors of power in Moscow. Russian leaders insisted on the implementation of the 21 February agreement and cast aspersions on the new government as illegitimate and put in place by an unconstitutional *coup d'état*.[32] The Russian ambassador to Ukraine was withdrawn. Putin and his advisers seem to have concluded that the collapse of the 21 February agreement resulted in part from a Western plot to install a loyal government in Kyiv that would move Ukraine toward the EU and even NATO. While no Western conspiracy in this simplistic form existed, the truth was not much better for Russia: individuals from the customary hotbeds of Ukrainian ethno-nationalism dominated the new administration; one in three ministers belonged to the far-right (and virulently anti-Russia) Svoboda party, and these authorities had come to power thanks in part to armed nationalist groups that still controlled government buildings in central Kyiv.

A spring snaps back

Within days, Russia struck back with a vengeance, as Putin set out to pry victory from the jaws of defeat by challenging the political order that had emerged after the Maidan Revolution. He had by this time run through all the standard plays in Russia's foreign-policy playbook with Ukraine: economic coercion (the trade war in July–September), lavish economic assistance (US$15bn in assistance for Yanukovych in December) and diplomacy with the West (the 21 February agreement). None of these had worked. So Putin reached for the only tool he had yet to deploy. To force the new Ukrainian authorities and the West to take Russia's interests into account, he decided to use the Russian military, now battle-ready after intensive reform and modernisation.

On or around 25 February 2014, special forces, paratroopers, and other men and materiel arrived in Crimea to bolster the sizeable contingent stationed there as part of the Black Sea Fleet, while other Russian forces deployed near the long land border with Ukraine and began large-scale drills. Russian commandos, the insignias removed from their uniforms, fanned out across the Crimean peninsula and began taking over Ukrainian military facilities and government buildings, including the Crimean parliament in the provincial capital of Simferopol, and setting up roadblocks.[33] On 1 March, Putin obtained unanimous approval from the upper house of Russia's parliament to deploy the armed forces on the territory of Ukraine 'until the normalisation of the socio-political situation' there.

If Putin had expected the invasion of Crimea and build-up along the border to force a return to something like the 21 February agreement, he was disappointed. Although the government in Kyiv was terrified, it refused a compromise on Russia's terms. When the speaker of the Russian lower house, Sergei Naryshkin, called Turchynov to convey an ultimatum from Putin, the acting Ukrainian president responded by calling Naryshkin a war criminal, rather than agreeing to concessions.[34] While holding out for the prospect of an 'off-ramp' (i.e., de-escalation) if Moscow pulled back its forces, Western governments focused on condemning Russian violations of Ukrainian borders and threatening consequences, eschewing high-level diplomacy with the Kremlin that might have defused the crisis.

Russia's incursion into Crimea had a raft of other unintended effects, setting off potent forces that among other things constrained its own policy. It emboldened pro-Russian politicians in Crimea and evoked latent separatist sentiment among the majority of the population on the peninsula. It also brought to the fore Russians' attachment to Crimea; surveys in 2013 had shown that more than half of Russian citizens considered Crimea to be part of Russia, not Ukraine.[35]

This combination of knock-on effects of the invasion led to an improvised annexation operation. In late February, the Crimean authorities, defying Kyiv, called a referendum on greater autonomy, to be held in May. Within less than a week, the date was moved forward twice and the question on the ballot changed. Voters were now asked whether they preferred to join Russia or remain part of Ukraine with enhanced prerogatives. While Putin had publicly reaffirmed Ukraine's territorial integrity as late as 4 March, within days the forces unleashed by the invasion left him with a choice of capitulation or annexation.[36]

In a hastily organised plebiscite conducted on 16 March with Russian special forces on guard near ballot stations, 97% of voters allegedly supported the option to join Russia, a result so preposterously lopsided as to further discredit the referendum, which was held in flagrant violation of the Ukrainian constitution. Moscow then moved quickly to incorporate the peninsula into Russia's federal system. Obama declared that the referendum would 'never be recognized by the United States and the international community', a statement that echoed widespread sentiment in the West.[37]

On 18 March, Putin delivered a blistering speech before a gathering of parliamentarians and political luminaries to announce Crimea's 'reunification' with Russia. He argued that the Soviet government's transfer of the peninsula to Ukrainian jurisdiction in 1954 had been illegal and arbitrary. In 1991, when Crimea became part of independent Ukraine, 'Russia felt that it was not simply robbed, it was plundered'. Russia, he said, had 'hung its head and resigned itself to this situation, swallowing its pride. Our country was going through such hard times then that it was incapable of protecting its interests. However, the people could not reconcile themselves to this outrageous historical injustice.' For years, the Russian government ignored their pleas. But, he said, 'everything has its limits'. After 'nationalists, neo-Nazis, Russophobes, and anti-Semites', with approval from the West, took power during the 'coup' in Kyiv, Russia had to act:

> In the case of Ukraine, our Western partners crossed the line, conducting themselves crudely, irresponsibly and unprofessionally. After all, they were fully aware that millions of Russians live in Ukraine and Crimea. They must have lost all their political instincts and even common sense not to foresee the consequences

of their actions. Russia was pushed to a point beyond which it could no longer retreat. If you compress a spring as tightly as possible, eventually it will snap back hard. You must always remember that.

Putin then launched into a diatribe against Western policies since the end of the Cold War, particularly the approach toward Russia and its neighbourhood:

> They have deceived us many times, made decisions behind our backs, placed us before faits accomplis. This happened with NATO's expansion to the east, as well as with the deployment of military infrastructure near our borders. They kept telling us the same thing: 'Well, this does not concern you.' Easy for them to say. … They are constantly trying to force us into a corner because we have independent policies, because we stand up for ourselves, because we call things like we see them and do not engage in hypocrisy. [38]

The Russian president had thrown down a gauntlet. Within a week, the ink was dry on the legal formalities of the annexation and all armed forces still loyal to Ukraine had left the peninsula (as many as two-thirds, beginning with the commander of the Ukrainian fleet there, defected to Russia).[39] In one fell swoop, Russia had rewritten the rules of the regional contestation, casting doubt on its broader relationship with the West and ties with its neighbours.

Whereas in the past it had allowed for notes of ambiguity and compromise, Russia now presented Western interlocutors with rough-edged demands. In crisis talks on 15 March, on the eve of the Crimea referendum, Foreign Minister Lavrov gave US Secretary of State John Kerry a draft text of a 'Friends of

Ukraine' international action plan.[40] The document contained five actionable points: the fulfilment of the pledges contained in the 21 February agreement to disband armed groups and de-occupy buildings; a new constitutional order for Ukraine, providing for, inter alia, neutrality, federalism and the direct election of oblast governments with significant new powers (including on economic policy and trade links with neighbouring countries); the elevation of Russian as an official state language along with Ukrainian; a new round of regional and national elections to take place after the constitutional reform; and recognition of the right to self-determination of the people of Crimea 'in accordance with the freely expressed will of its population as manifest in the 16 March referendum'. There were to be EU, US and Russian guarantees of all the above, which was to be codified in a resolution of the UN Security Council. The core objectives – neutrality, undisturbed economic ties with Russia and 'federalisation' of Ukraine to ensure the pro-Russian oblasts have a veto over decision-making in Kyiv – have remained unchanged ever since. The Russians now wanted ironclad guarantees regarding Ukraine's geopolitical and geo-economic future. Rejecting the West's geo-ideational emphasis on the unalloyed right to choose, Russia wanted the deal clinched by the great powers and imposed on Ukraine.

Doubling down

In the wake of the Crimea annexation, the West and Russia effectively doubled down on the very policies that had precipitated the crisis in the first place. The annexation had failed to further Moscow's objectives as set out in Lavrov's action plan of 15 March 2014. So Russia seized on a wave of anti-Maidan, anti-government protests that were now breaking out across southern and eastern Ukraine. After local activists, many of them voicing separatist slogans, seized administrative buildings in Donetsk, Luhansk and several smaller towns in the two eponymous oblasts, declaring themselves the Donetsk People's Republic (DNR) and Luhansk People's Republic (LNR), the Ukrainian government ordered a military assault on them under the banner of an 'anti-terrorist operation'. Initially, it was haphazard and underpowered, leaving volunteer paramilitary battalions to take the lead. A motley crew of Russian civilian volunteers along with special forces and operatives streamed across the border, adding fuel to the fire. The Kremlin also turned up the economic heat by rescinding not only the gas discount accorded to Yanukovych in December but the earlier price cut traded for the extension of the lease on the Black Sea Fleet base in 2010, and demanding prepayment for the following month's gas delivery.

Russia continued playing the military card. The border-area drills were transformed into a sustained build-up of a strike force estimated at the better part of 50,000 strong. Russia could now invade its neighbour at a moment's notice. It also sent more sophisticated weapons across the border. Anti-aircraft systems proved particularly lethal, leading to the grounding of the Ukrainian air force after several planes were shot down. Russia was resorting to increasingly destructive means to get its way.

Kremlin statements telegraphed an interest in sowing chaos. In mid-April, Putin declared, 'We believe that we ought to do everything we can to help these people [in southern and eastern Ukraine] defend their rights and independently determine their fate. ... The essential issue is how to ensure the legitimate rights and interests of ethnic Russians and Russian speakers in the south and east of Ukraine.' He 'reminded' the audience that the Donbas and other oblasts were part of the Russian Empire, and 'were given to Ukraine in the 1920s by the Soviet government. Why they did this, God only knows.'[41] Russia was unsubtly egging on anti-Maidan sentiment and encouraging destabilisation. Given the implications of Putin's questioning of ownership rights over much of Ukraine's south and east, the build-up on the border, and the lightning-fast evolution of the Crimea operation, neither Kyiv nor Western capitals could have any degree of certainty about Moscow's next move.

In the meantime, the US and the EU stepped up support for the newly installed authorities in Kyiv. Days after the revolution, NATO agreed on measures to bolster its partnership with Ukraine. Obama received Yatsenyuk at the White House, a first for a Ukrainian prime minister, and pledged backing for his government, including a US$1bn loan guarantee and nearly US$200m in aid. Vice President Biden soon flew to Kyiv, the first of several visits, to reinforce US support for Ukraine as the government mounted the counter-attack against the separatists.

The EU granted Ukraine preferential access to its markets, a unilateral implementation of the EU's commitments to lower tariffs under the DCFTA. By removing 95% of EU customs duties on imports of industrial goods from Ukraine and all tariffs on agricultural produce, Brussels was effectively granting hundreds of millions of euros of assistance. The EU also provided significant transfers to the Ukrainian government budget. By the end of June, Kyiv had signed the AA. Most importantly, the International Monetary Fund (IMF) approved US$17bn in loans for Ukraine.[42] A first instalment of more than US$3bn was made available immediately, shoring up the country's accounts.

The declared strategic goal of all of this support was to create a reformed, secure and Western-integrated Ukraine. In other words, the plan was to deepen previous policies in order to create what the Kremlin would inevitably consider a geopolitical and geo-economic defeat in Ukraine. From the Kremlin's perspective, in the aftermath of the Crimean annexation the US

and EU had declared their intention to recreate the very conditions that led Moscow to invade the peninsula in late February.

Concurrently, the West and Russia began a sanctions war.
There was a diplomatic push to isolate Russia, including by
kicking the country out of the G8 grouping, shutting down the
NATO–Russia Council and suspending EU–Russia summits. The
day after the Crimea referendum, the US and the EU (followed
soon afterwards by Norway, Switzerland, Canada and Australia)
began the first in a series of economic-sanction designations for
individuals and corporate entities.[43] The individuals' assets were
frozen, transactions with them were made unlawful and they
were banned from travel to the sanctioning country or group of
countries. The individuals sanctioned included several groups:
a range of Russian officials, military officers, MPs and tycoons
considered close to Putin; Russian-appointed functionaries in
Crimea; members of the former Yanukovych government; and
leaders of the DNR and LNR. Sanctioned entities – initially
Crimea-based firms and a range of companies, including several
banks, majority-owned by sanctioned individuals – had their
assets frozen, and sanctioning-country-based firms were barred
from doing business with them. The list of sanctioned individuals and entities grew into the triple digits by 2016. Within a week
of the first sanctions announcement, the now G7 and the EU
threatened to move to general sector-wide restrictions on Russia
if Moscow continued to destabilise eastern Ukraine.[44] Markets
and investors were forced to price in the risk that governments
would act on the threat. The rouble and the Russian stock-market
index dropped precipitously. The US subsequently announced
a suspension of licensing for exports and re-exports to Russia of
defence and dual-use items.[45]

The stated purpose of these salvos was, Obama said, 'not
to punish Russia; the goal is to give them an incentive to
choose the better course, and that is to resolve these issues

diplomatically'.[46] From the Kremlin, the sanctions looked more like economic warfare intended to inflict pain and even destabilise the country. It was true that some of the choices of targets were hard to square with Obama's dictum. The very first US sanctions list included, in addition to Ukrainians and Russians involved in the crisis, the MP who authored a notorious 2012 law banning the adoption of Russian children by Americans but had nothing to do with Ukraine. The belligerent language some US officials used cemented the view in Moscow that Washington wanted to hurt Russia, not help Ukraine. In testimony before the US Senate about the sanctions, Assistant Secretary of State Victoria Nuland warned that 'unless Putin changes course, at some point in the not-too-distant future, the current nationalistic fever will break in Russia'. 'When it does', she went on, 'it will give way to a sweaty and harsh realization of the economic costs. ... Russia's citizens will ask: What have we really achieved? Instead of funding schools, hospitals, science, and prosperity at home in Russia, we have squandered our national wealth on adventurism, interventionism, and the ambitions of a leader who cares more about empire than his own citizens.'[47] Many in the Russian elite, as Sergei Karaganov of the Higher School of Economics in Moscow put it, considered this 'a de facto declaration of political war'.[48]

As the conflict in eastern Ukraine intensified, the US imposed sanctions that were harsher and more sophisticated than previous measures. In July 2014, the Treasury Department prohibited the financing of debt with a maturity of more than 90 days for several large Russian banks. It was initially unclear whether Brussels would follow suit, as Europe's extensive economic ties with Russia meant that the blowback from sanctions would be significantly greater for EU member states. Yet the downing of a Malaysia Airlines passenger jet over the Donbas on 17 July altered the political dynamic in Europe. As best we know, flight MH17 was shot down either by a Russian army unit or by rebels who thought they were targeting a Ukrainian military plane.

Putin's lack of contrition and the various denials of culpability by the Russian government forced the EU governments' hand. A week after the crash, Brussels imposed similar limits on Russian financial institutions' access to European capital markets, banning the export of defence and dual-use technology to Russia and keeping the country from acquiring 'sensitive technologies' in the oil sector. Over the following weeks, the US and the EU added several financial institutions to the debt-maturity limits list and tightened the limits from 90 to 30 days. The US also issued a supplementary directive forbidding the export of goods, services and technology 'in support of exploration or production for deepwater, Arctic offshore, or shale projects' in Russia.[49] The EU soon matched this step. As a result, ExxonMobil announced in September that it would wind down its operations in the Kara Sea, where the company had been participating in a joint venture with Russian state-owned energy company Rosneft. Economic ties between Russia and the West built up meticulously over 25 years were rent asunder in a matter of months.

On 7 August 2014, Russia reacted with an import ban on agricultural goods and foodstuffs from the US, the EU and other countries that had imposed restrictive measures on it. These sanctions were enacted under the aegis of 'import substitution', an idea that became a rallying cry for Russian officialdom with the domestic audience. While the ban provided new opportunities for some Russian producers, its main effect in the short term was inflationary. It also hit the bottom line of the politically well-connected agricultural sector in Europe.

Much like the interaction in the region between Russia and the West before 2014, the diplomatic response to the Ukraine crisis was almost an afterthought. Following their meeting in March, Kerry and Lavrov did not reconvene until a month later when, with the EU's Ashton and the acting Ukrainian foreign minister, they issued a joint statement in Geneva calling for an end to the carnage in the Donbas.[50] Regrettably, the statement had no impact on the fighting. With the exception of leader-level and minister-level phone calls, the only events during the next four months that resembled negotiations were side meetings during the 70th anniversary of D-Day in early June.

When talks did occur, little progress was made. Western leaders, pushing their geo-ideational case, argued that the root cause of the crisis was Russia's aggression against Ukraine that had begun in late February when its people made their choice for a new political order. The West demanded an end to Russia's belligerence and expected it to respect the will of the Ukrainian people. There was no appetite to negotiate with Moscow about that. As Obama said in July 2014:

> The sooner the Russians recognize that the best chance for them to have influence inside of Ukraine is by being good neighbors and maintaining trade and commerce, rather than trying to dictate what the Ukrainian people can aspire to, rendering Ukraine a vassal state to Russia ... the sooner we can resolve this crisis.[51]

He and the Europeans insisted on a cessation of Russian aid to the rebels and a pullback of the Russian troops now deployed along the border. While legally and morally justified, this demand was not a viable basis for talks; Moscow was not going to comply, since doing so would have allowed Ukrainian government forces to crush the insurgency. Russia was not prepared to permit the restoration of government control in the Donbas until it got a deal along the lines of the 15 March document. And neither the West nor Kyiv was willing to negotiate on these terms. While abjuring such a compromise, the West was also – understandably – not ready to escalate to the level required to shake Russia's determination to pursue its objectives.

Russia's actions in this period constituted a major roadblock to a diplomatic resolution of the crisis. The annexation of Crimea and stoking of the insurgency in eastern Ukraine not only made dealing with Moscow an order of magnitude more politically fraught; it also forced a reassessment of Russia's intentions in the West. Western leaders began to question whether Putin's ambitions extended beyond Ukraine; Russia's unpredictability was now seen as a huge security problem for the West itself. Uncertainty about Russia's intentions was compounded by the cognitive dissonance in the interactions between Russian officials and their Western counterparts. By late spring, it became clear that talks at the ministerial level were largely pointless. Two days after signing the Geneva joint statement in April, Lavrov repudiated the document and his Western negotiating partners in an English-language interview.[52] US officials drew the conclusion that his 'wings had been clipped' because he had not been given a clear mandate and had unwittingly crossed a red line.[53] A similar scenario unfolded after Economic Development Minister Aleksei Ulyukaev made a concession in talks on Ukraine's DCFTA that autumn.[54] Putin had reduced the decision-making group on Ukraine to himself and a few close advisers.

But talking directly to Putin also yielded little. The Ukrainian, US and EU leaders wanted to discuss a pull-out of Russian troops and an end to the conflict in the Donbas; Putin consistently denied that there were any Russian soldiers in Ukraine. He was likely doing so to maintain the veneer of legality and to give himself a way of withdrawing without retreating.

Putin's two main opposite numbers, Obama and Merkel, were infuriated by what they saw as his lies and penchant for long-winded tirades. Both are result-oriented, pragmatic politicians. So when Obama's phone calls with Putin were dominated by complaints about threats to Russian speakers in eastern Ukraine from what the Russian president called the 'fascists' in Kyiv, and Merkel's tête-à-tête with him at a G20 meeting began with a two-hour litany of Western betrayals, both began to lose interest in further dialogue.[55] However, Putin was not simply being obstructionist. He wanted to talk to Obama and Merkel about a new geopolitical and geo-economic settlement for Ukraine, and perhaps the regional architecture more broadly. They wanted Russia out of Ukraine. In other words, there was no common ground.

With other leaders, Putin was outspoken and even thuggish. In August, he told Ukrainian President Petro Poroshenko (who had been inaugurated in June) that 'if he really wanted to invade, he had 1.2m soldiers armed with the world's most sophisticated weaponry. They could be in Kyiv in two days – or in Tallinn, Vilnius, Riga, and Bucharest.'[56] In a call with Barroso the following month, he employed similarly inflammatory rhetoric, reportedly saying he could 'take Kyiv in two weeks' if he wanted to do so.[57] While there was some truth to Putin's statements, and one can sense the frustration that must have prompted them, the effect was to aggravate tensions.

Without the prospect of a diplomatic resolution, Moscow had to significantly increase its involvement on the battlefield, since its rebel proxies in the Donbas were increasingly outmanned and outgunned. By the end of August, the Ukrainians were about to encircle the two oblast capitals and retake border crossings, which would have finished off the insurgency. The US administration was split between those who feared Russia would respond to such a move with overwhelming force and others who were 'saying [the Ukrainian forces] should take one of those towns and then sue for peace, to prove to [Putin] that he can't win'.[58] While the debate between these groups raged inside the Washington Beltway, the US was effectively sitting on the sidelines, neither deploying its significant leverage to push the Ukrainians to end the offensive nor encouraging them to continue it.

Just as the separatist forces seemed on their last legs, Russia intervened more directly. Backed by the Russian military, including artillery shelling from across the border and a 3,000-troop reinforcement, the separatists counter-attacked, moving south and capturing towns and cities towards the Sea of Azov. Ukraine's army suffered a calamitous setback in the town of Ilovaisk, when its forces were caught in a pincer by units wielding advanced weaponry, widely assumed to be Russian regulars. Hundreds of Ukrainian soldiers were killed or went missing.

The Russian hammer blow made it clear to Kyiv that outright military victory over the separatists was impossible. It more than anything drove the Ukrainians to the negotiating table – or, strictly speaking, the long-distance telephone, as Poroshenko and Putin hashed out a deal in several hours-long conversations in late August and early September. It was formalised in a 12-point protocol signed in Minsk on 5 September. The agreement called for, inter alia, a ceasefire monitored by the OSCE; the decentralisation of power within Ukraine, one point of which would be a law on 'special status' for rebel-held areas of the Donbas, giving them powers similar to those called for in the document of 15 March; a permanent OSCE presence along the Ukraine–Russia border; release of all hostages and prisoners; an amnesty law for combatants; early local elections in rebel-held areas; and the withdrawal of unauthorised armed groups and equipment. Together with a more detailed memorandum signed later that month, this set of arrangements came to be known as Minsk I. The basic trade was peace and withdrawal for Ukraine's acceptance of the central demands of the Russian 15 March document.

Although many of the provisions of Minsk I were never put into effect, it did prompt a sharp decline in violence, from 756 fatalities, or 42 people per day, in the 18 days before the agreement was signed, to 331 deaths in the month following, or about 11 per day.[59] Hundreds of captives were also exchanged. Nonetheless, fighting continued in hotspots like the Donetsk airport, and both sides used the respite to reinforce their positions on the front lines. None of the political components of the deal were implemented, while endless diplomatic conclaves debated the meaning of the vague commitments that had been made. Moscow decided to force the issue again in early 2015, when the separatists, backed by a second direct Russian intervention, once again forced Ukrainian government troops to flee. By early February the separatists had gained control over an additional 300 sq km of terrain, including what was left of the Donetsk airport.

In a bid to end the renewed violence and avert a broader war, Merkel and French President François Hollande visited Kyiv and Moscow in early February to lay the groundwork for new talks, which were held in Minsk on 11–12 February. After 16 hours of non-stop negotiations, Poroshenko, Putin, Merkel and Hollande finalised a list of 'implementing measures' to enact the principles of Minsk I. This 13-point document came to be known as Minsk II.

Stalemate

The new deal overlapped significantly with Minsk I. But it reflected the separatists' and Russians' gains on the battlefield, which Putin used to garner several key concessions from

Poroshenko. Reform of the Ukrainian constitution was made the lynchpin of the peace process. Furthermore, the agreement was much more specific than the earlier document about how to sequence the provisions. In particular, Russia would only have to return control of rebel-held areas of the border after Ukraine ratified the constitutional amendments.

Minsk II had serious shortcomings. In the field, the most significant were the lack of an agreed armistice line and an effective instrument to enforce the ceasefire and weapons withdrawal. The OSCE monitoring effort was, by design, not a peacekeeping mission, in contrast with initiatives in analogous conflict zones. Staffed by unarmed civilians and not uniformed military personnel, it was unable to ensure compliance.

These shortcomings manifested themselves almost immediately in the battle for Debaltseve, a transportation hub between Donetsk and Luhansk cities. Five days after Minsk II, Ukrainian government troops took heavy losses in a haphazard exit from the town. Estimates of casualties varied, ranging from one dozen to hundreds, and 100 or more Ukrainian soldiers were taken prisoner. The UN reported that 500 civilians were found dead in their homes.[60] Following the capture of Debaltseve and surrounding territory by the separatists, there has been a stable 'line of contact' demarcating rebel-controlled from government-controlled areas. It is a jagged semicircle bounded by the Russian border to the east and tracing far north of Luhansk city, northwest of Horlivka and Donetsk city, and west of Novoazovsk, on the Sea of Azov (see map on p. 16). It marked off slightly less than one-third of the territory of the two oblasts.

While violence did subsequently subside, the conflict-resolution process soon stalled. The stalemate resulted from divergent understandings of where the process should lead. For the Kremlin, Minsk II represented the practical implementation of Moscow's stated objective of reworking Ukraine's institutions in order to cement Russian influence over Kyiv, thereby denying the West geopolitical, geo-economic and geo-ideational victory. Minsk II itemised the enhanced rights for the separatist areas (such as circumscribing Kyiv's control over law enforcement there) and compelled Kyiv to negotiate a constitutional reform with the separatists that codifies autonomy for their fiefdoms inside Ukraine. Based on the published version of the constitutional amendments proposed by the separatist negotiators, all of the same demands in the 15 March document, including neutrality and enhanced status for the Russian language, were still alive.[61]

Ukraine, having committed through its president to some form of this outcome at Minsk, has refused to follow through on it. Only the parliamentary opposition, mostly one-time members of Yanukovych's Party of Regions, has voiced support for fulfilling Minsk II in its entirety. Denunciations of the agreement as unsatisfactory or even treasonous have been far more commonplace among the political elite. Some favoured biding time until the Donbas can be retaken by force, a scenario referred to as the 'Croatian option', a reference to Croatia's forceful retaking of the Srpska Krajina in 1995. Others said Ukraine should press forward with some elements of Minsk II, but only enough to disprove claims that Kyiv is responsible for its failure.[62]

In the short term, Kyiv's tacit preference was for a frozen conflict: dodging the political aspects of Minsk II, but ending the active fighting while severing rebel-held Donbas from the rest of the polity. In this scenario, the line of contact would become a de facto border, like the inner German border during the Cold War. The influence of the Donbas over politics in the capital would be eliminated, and thus Moscow's sway over Kyiv would be minimised. Russia would have to foot the bill for the reconstruction effort and for the costs of preventing a socio-economic implosion in its new protectorate.

The problem for Kyiv is that this frozen-conflict scenario is a non-starter for Moscow. As an authoritative Russian political insider put it, 'To get Donbas and lose Ukraine represents a defeat for the Kremlin. In that case, it would be better not to have started [supporting the insurgency] in the first place.'[63] Following this logic, Russia has kept up its support for the armed rebels in the Donbas – and for the region's civilians – while increasing its command and control. This led, as of late 2016, to a conflict more aptly described as simmering than frozen, defined by continuous low-level fighting punctuated by periodic upticks in violence. The ensuing security challenge overloaded the Ukrainian government's political bandwidth and absorbed a disproportionate share of an already hard-pressed budget. As a result, the Ukrainian economy remained in disarray, and few investors had the fortitude to return. But Moscow calibrated the fighting so as not to spark an all-out war or a more forceful Western response.

By supporting the Donbas insurgency, Russia has effectively been able to keep Ukraine off-kilter. But it is no closer to getting the political settlement it wants. Despite several follow-up Russia–France–Germany–Ukraine summits and numerous ministerial meetings, the most concrete result since the signing of Minsk II was an agreement in December 2015 to extend the deadline for implementation of the deal into 2016. The package of constitutional reforms that would partially fulfil the central political requirement has not made it through the Ukrainian parliament and there is no agreement on procedures for conducting local elections in the conflict zone. Moreover, the amnesty provision has not been passed, and Kyiv has enforced an economic blockade of separatist territory, as well as severe restrictions on freedom of movement across the line of contact.

An embattled Poroshenko is loath to expend political capital on unpopular steps that would end up empowering the Donbas, the traditional stronghold of his political opponents.

The domestic stalemate in Ukraine resonates with an international stalemate. The war and Kyiv's dysfunction have nullified any immediate risk to Russia of losing Ukraine to the West, the worst-case scenario that had driven its behaviour. Yet neither Russia nor the West has made a good-faith effort to find common ground on the geopolitical and geo-economic conflict over Ukraine's trajectory. US and European officials continue to declare their support for Ukraine's 'European future', while the NATO and EU bureaucracies busily deepen integration with Kyiv. While there is no momentum for formal membership offers in the short term from either organisation, the possibility of such an offer in the future is explicitly still in play, even if that future is a distant one. Moscow, of course, seeks to rule out such a possibility and roll back the integration that has already occurred. Therefore, even if Minsk II can somehow be implemented, the core contestation between Russia and the West over Ukraine will be no closer to resolution.

Neither side has sought an inclusive, negotiated settlement. The negotiations that did take place concerned the minutiae of the several Minsk agreements. But disputes over details such as the rules governing local elections in the Donbas are really proxies for the broader conflict that remains unaddressed. At an October 2014 meeting of EU leaders, Poroshenko and Putin in Milan (after Minsk I but before Minsk II), Merkel pushed the Russian president to commit to hold local elections under Ukrainian law, silence the rebel guns and hand back control over the border. Putin balked, claiming that both sides were failing to make good on their commitments. Poroshenko objected, and the EU leaders took his side. Predictably, the meeting ended in failure, with the EU and Russia blaming each other.[64] Barring a high-level effort to address the first-order issues, such meetings cannot produce breakthroughs. Even full implementation of Minsk II would in effect allow the conflict to continue without the use of military force.

Indeed, in parallel to the war in the east, the geo-economic contest between the EU and Russia over Ukraine continued in meeting chambers in various capital cities. On 26 August 2014, just before the first direct Russian intervention in the Donbas, EU leaders gathered with the presidents of Russia, Ukraine, Kazakhstan and Belarus for talks in Minsk. The formal agenda of the meeting was to address the conflict over Ukraine's DCFTA with the EU. Putin kept many of his public remarks focused on this very point, alleging grave consequences from the DCFTA for Russia–Ukraine trade ties. He said:

> Russia has stated on numerous occasions that full acceptance by our Ukrainian friends of all the tariff liberalisation requirements and the adoption of the European Union's technical, food safety and veterinary norms will have a negative impact on the scope and dynamics of trade and investment cooperation in Eurasia. By very conservative estimates, the total loss for the economy of Russia alone may amount to 100 billion roubles during the first stage, that is $3 billion. This will affect entire sectors of our economy and agriculture, with all the attendant consequences for economic growth and employment rates.[65]

He went on to explain that Moscow would take steps to protect its economy should these concerns go unaddressed.

Once the cameras were off, Putin made his position clear: besides altering the standards, 2,340 tariff lines in the DCFTA would have to be changed. The EU trade commissioner, Karel

De Gucht, repeatedly rebutted Putin's arguments about the injury Russia would suffer from the DCFTA.[66] He and other EU leaders were sure that Putin's demands were a ploy to scuttle the deal.[67] They also had a parochial bureaucratic interest in rejecting Putin's arguments. Altering just one tariff line – let alone 2,340 – would require the Commission to obtain a new mandate, necessitating a painstaking renegotiation among the 28 member states. This rigidity is a common feature of the EU's international trade negotiations. It creates strong disincentives to amend course midstream, even when doing so would be sensible, as it was in this case.

Later, Putin asked Poroshenko to put off ratification of the deal in order to allow more time for talks. Poroshenko agreed to talks, but stood his ground on proceeding with ratification less than a month later. The Russian military's assault on his forces that ended in the defeat at Ilovaisk on 2 September 2014 changed Poroshenko's mind. In addition to agreeing to Minsk I, he also conceded to Putin's demand to reopen the text of the AA to change the DCFTA. He presented this compromise to NATO leaders at their summit in Wales a few days later. 'Mr Obama responded first, according to a person in the room. Was this something Ukraine wanted, or Mr Putin wanted? Mr Poroshenko made clear he was the one seeking it. Mr Obama turned to Ms Merkel: if the Ukrainians want it, why not? She agreed.' But even Obama and Merkel were not prepared to take on the EU's institutional unwillingness to revisit the AA. When they presented the compromise to Barroso, he was 'incredulous'. 'Barroso was, like, WTF?' a US official recalled. Invoking the Maidan Revolution as evidence of what could happen if Poroshenko agreed to a renegotiation, Barroso, 'desperate to find a way to keep the [AA] on track', talked Obama and Merkel into renouncing the Ukrainian president's deal with Putin and allowing ratification of the agreement to proceed.[68] In place of a renegotiation, the EU would ratify the AA but offer Russia a 15-month pause in implementation of the trade-related parts of the agreement, during which time fuller explanations and technical tweaks would be possible, but not substantive amendments.

EU commissioner De Gucht was to present this modified deal to Russia the following week. In the run-up to the meeting, the Russian government sent Brussels and Kyiv its proposals for the talks, which the latter duly leaked to a Ukrainian newspaper. The 59-page document called for extensive changes to the DCFTA, in accordance with Putin's earlier demands, not trifling misunderstandings about the text that the EU could simply clarify.[69]

The EU, in short, was fully aware that Moscow was expecting a renegotiation when the Russian minister Ulyukaev arrived in Brussels for the talks. De Gucht rejected the Russian proposal categorically and aired the 15-month pause offer. He told Ulyukaev that 'the decision was simple: either we have a deal on the 15-month plan or we don't. There would be no further compromise.' Ulyukaev, in a move that would see him reprimanded upon his return home, agreed. One EU official involved in the talks celebrated the result: '[Russia's] purpose was to delay the thing until doomsday and break it open on substance. On both counts, they failed.'[70] The two sides were still locked into their zero-sum geo-economic competition.

Moscow quickly walked back Ulyukaev's concession. Putin wrote in a letter to EU officials that they could either agree to renegotiation of the DCFTA, or else Moscow would follow through on its threat to suspend the CIS free-trade arrangements and hike tariffs on Ukrainian exports to Russia. 'We still believe that only systemic adjustments of the [DCFTA], which take into account the full range of risks to Russian–Ukrainian economic ties and to the whole Russian economy arising from implementation of the agreement, will allow [us] to retain [the] existing trade and economic [regime] between the Russian Federation and Ukraine', he wrote.[71] The 15-month hiatus was a 'period of clarification', as the EU's De Gucht put it, the purpose of which was to allow the EU to demonstrate to Russia that it had no reason to worry.[72] Russia and the EU were seeking geo-economic victory, not a compromise solution.

After 12 rounds of negotiations over 15 months, the talks unsurprisingly broke down at a final meeting in late December 2015. Russia reiterated its demand for a legally binding document to address its concerns and stated its intention to suspend the CIS trade arrangements vis-à-vis Ukraine. The EU accused Russia of putting forth 'requests that were not substantiated' and ruled out further talks until Moscow committed to holding tariffs on Ukraine steady. The Commission also issued a document in order to debunk 'certain myths' – that is, Russia's objections to the DCFTA. The EU further reminded Russia that it never intended to compromise: 'As has been conveyed from the beginning of the talks … the DCFTA cannot be amended – neither directly nor indirectly.' In Putin's account, the Russian delegation was told, '"The game is up". [The EU delegation] then left [the room] and issued a press release [saying] that the Russian side broke off the talks', a step he lamented as 'not very European'.[73]

A number of Western analysts have joined the EU's trade negotiators in pronouncing the concerns Russia raised during the trilateral talks groundless, and concluding that therefore Moscow must have other, hidden motives.[74] This explanation, while not necessarily inaccurate, relies on inference rather than evidence; the Russian negotiators could have been sincere but mistaken. The broader point is that the EU and Ukraine wanted to deepen their geo-economic integration without Russian involvement, and Moscow was not prepared to continue to extend preferential trade arrangements to Ukraine under these circumstances. While it seemed as if Ukraine's president was prepared for a compromise on the DCFTA when he arrived at the Wales summit, the EU – for institutional-bureaucratic reasons – insisted the text could not be altered.

When the DCFTA went into effect on 1 January 2016, Russia suspended the CIS trade preferences accorded to Ukraine, effectively instituting a punitive tariff hike. Moscow also placed an embargo on Ukrainian agricultural imports similar to its countersanctions against the G7. In response, Kyiv banned a variety of Russian imports including meat, fish, vegetables, fruit, dairy and alcohol products. Taken together with tit-for-tat sanctions that cut direct air links between the countries (affecting up to 70,000 passengers per month), by 2016 Russian–Ukrainian economic ties had been almost completely severed. And the geo-economic stalemate was more intractable than ever.

The negative-sum game and how to move past it

Everyone loses

The crux of our argument is that the Ukraine crisis is the apotheosis of a broader regional dynamic: zero-sum policies producing negative-sum results. It is a game that has produced no winners. All major players are worse off today than they were when the crisis began.

Ukraine, the central battleground, has been hit the hardest. It has lost control over the Crimean peninsula and over a population there of more than 2m.[1] Pro-Russian Crimeans might have rejoiced in their new-found freedom from the Ukrainian government; the euphoria was short-lived. The peninsula's status as a subunit of Russia is internationally unrecognised, hotly contested by Western states and ergo reversible. The most draconian of the US and EU sanctions, and probably the most lasting, have been imposed on economic interaction with Crimea. They are as stringent as those once levied on Iran: not only are Western firms forbidden from investing or trading, but even Russian firms that conduct business in the US or EU are effectively barred from operating there.[2] Budgetary injections from Moscow have been offset by rampant inflation caused by the Ukrainian blockade on exports to Crimea, the cutting off of irrigation water for agriculture, and blackouts following the severing of electrical lines on the Perekop isthmus joining the peninsula to the mainland.[3] Along with these economic challenges, the OSCE reports that the 'human rights and fundamental freedoms' of Crimeans are being abridged.[4] Amnesty International documents widespread abuses by the Russian authorities, including 'a series of abductions and torture of their critics' and an 'unrelenting campaign of intimidation' against independent media and groups speaking for the Crimean Tatars, the Muslim minority population that was deported by Stalin and spent more than 40 years in exile.[5]

The takeover of Crimea was bloodless, but the fighting in the Donbas, as noted in the Introduction, has claimed approximately 10,000 lives. Some 1.8m Ukrainians have been displaced internally, while nearly 1.1m have registered as refugees in Russia.[6] This latter number significantly understates flight to Russia since by all accounts most Ukrainians who did so have not gone through the formal registration process, preferring simply to find work or shelter with relatives.

The humanitarian impact goes beyond the tragedies of death and displacement. The UN, the OSCE and human-rights groups have documented widespread violations in the conflict zone committed by the Russia-backed rebels and by the Ukrainian government and paramilitary forces. 'Both the Ukrainian government authorities and Russia-backed separatists in eastern Ukraine', report Amnesty International and Human Rights Watch, 'have held civilians in prolonged, arbitrary detention, without any contact with the outside world. … Most of those detained suffered torture or other forms of ill-treatment.'[7] The Office of the UN High Commissioner for Human Rights (OHCHR) has reported 'a pattern of cases of [the Security Service of Ukraine] detaining and … torturing the female relatives of men suspected of membership or affiliation with ... armed [separatist] groups'.[8] No less repugnantly, separatist forces have 'imposed an arbitrary system of rules, established a network of places of deprivation of liberty where detainees are tortured and ill-treated, and cracked down on dissent' in areas under their control.[9] The term 'Donetsk basement' became synonymous in 2014 and 2015 with makeshift subterranean prisons and torture chambers, where those suspected of pro-Maidan sympathies or other heretical views were held incommunicado.[10]

The lives of many rank-and-file Ukrainians in the conflict zone have been turned upside down by all that has happened. In government-controlled stretches of Donetsk and Luhansk, where livelihoods had depended on ties with the provincial capitals now under rebel control, economic activity has contracted steeply. And the tightening of the security regime at the line of contact has made crossing it an exorbitantly time-consuming activity, with queueing often taking 24 hours or more. In mid-2016, OHCHR stated that 'Ukrainian authorities have often run afoul of the principle of non-discrimination through adopting policies that distinguish, exclude, and restrict access to fundamental freedoms and socio-economic rights to persons living in the conflict-affected area.'[11] Within the separatist territories, shortages of goods, and black markets, wage arrears and lawlessness are among the hardships of daily life. Since the start of the conflict, separatists have taken over at least 50 state-owned mines and looted Ukrainian- and foreign-owned businesses.[12]

For the country as a whole, the economic burden of the conflict and the revolution that preceded it has been extremely heavy. The World Bank reports that GDP contracted by 7% in 2014, only to fall by 10% in 2015. The Bank forecasted that the economy could grow by 1% in 2016 in a best-case scenario involving peace and progress on reform, but even that is merely the result of what economists call base effects, that is, an economy can only go up after hitting rock bottom. Ukrainians have been pummelled by inflation, with consumer prices rising 25% in 2014 and a whopping 43% in 2015. Industrial output dropped by 20% in 2014 and 13% in 2015. The currency has lost more than 60% of its value against the dollar since 2014. As the conflict in the east drags on, the economic domino effects can only get worse. As Ukraine's heartland for mining and metallurgy, the Donbas accounted for 16% of the country's GDP, 25% of industrial output and 27% of exports in 2013, the year before the conflict. Predictably, the nationwide macroeconomic downturn has seriously complicated the lives of ordinary people. Household expenditures were down by 20% in 2015, reflecting cutbacks in spending on food and other necessities; the calorific content of food consumed fell by 18% on average.[13] A Gallup poll in late 2015 reported that 79% of Ukrainians viewed the country's economic situation as 'poor', while only 9% reported that they were thriving, compared with around 56% who said they were struggling and 36% who were suffering.[14]

One formidable source of economic distress has been the rupturing of commercial ties with Ukraine's giant neighbour, Russia. Thus far, the contraction of Ukraine's GDP, and particularly the collapse of energy-intensive industries in the east, has dampened demand for Russian gas. If and when its economy recovers, Ukraine will have little alternative to re-establishing the gas relationship with Russia. 'Reverse flow' of Russian gas from Europe has helped Ukraine get through the past few years, but all possible pipelines operating at full capacity can currently provide Ukraine with no more than 12bn cubic metres (bcm) a year; in 2013, Ukraine imported 27bcm of Russian gas.[15] In the past, the gas relationship with Russia was a key source of fiscal stability. In 2013 Gazprom poured

US$3.1bn in transit fees into Ukrainian coffers, a sizeable percentage of gross state revenue. With alternative pipelines from Russia to Europe that bypass Ukraine via the Black and Baltic seas coming online in the next few years, the future of Kyiv's gas-transit income is in doubt.

Ukraine's structural dependency on Russia is not confined to gas imports and transit. One-third of its total exports went to Russia in pre-crisis 2013, or about the same as to the EU. By the Ukrainian government's own estimates, it lost US$98bn in trade in 2014 and 2015 from sanctions imposed by Russia.[16] The net effect is significantly greater because of the composition of Ukraine's exports. It mostly sells metal ore, ferrous metals, and grain and other agricultural goods to Europe. To Russia, by contrast, it has exported machinery, transport services and industrial products – that is, value-added goods and services that tend to provide more and higher-paying jobs.[17] Several huge enterprises, mainly in the defence and aerospace industry, had only Russian clients before the crisis. Kept afloat for now by subsidies and pre-existing contracts, they will soon either go bankrupt or have to be retooled. The Yuzhmash plant in Dnipro (formerly Dnipropetrovsk), which has subsisted since 1991 mostly by producing and servicing missiles for Russia, now works only one day a week and owes millions of dollars in back wages to its workers; the Antonov firm in Kyiv, which had produced large cargo planes jointly with a Russian partner, suspended production in March 2016.

While undergoing economic and conflict-related pain, Ukrainians have seen only modest improvements in governance since the Maidan Revolution. Several significant reforms have been enacted, but day-to-day realities in Ukraine have changed little, despite the soaring rhetoric often used by Ukrainian officials and their Western backers. National polls conducted in late 2015 found that nearly 80% of Ukrainians believed that the level of corruption was the same as or worse than before the revolution. Only 8% of Ukrainians had confidence in the national government, just 19% said the country was headed in the right direction, and Petro Poroshenko's presidential approval rating fell to an abysmal 17%, ten points lower than Viktor Yanukovych's on the eve of his overthrow.[18]

Ukrainian politics have also become more polarised and rife with extreme discourse and behaviour. National identity, it is true, has been vigorously contested ever since the country's independence in 1991. Divergent visions of culture, history and language set apart many in the south and east from those in the west and centre. Given the highly centralised nature of the Ukrainian government, those in charge in Kyiv have always had the power to impose their views on the rest of the country. Before 2014, though, factionalism and disorganisation within the Verkhovna Rada and executive branch prevented any single part of the country from locking in total dominance. The Maidan Revolution marked a qualitative shift in this regard. As noted above, far-right nationalists were the armed vanguard of the uprising, and the post-revolutionary government was dominated by representatives of western portions of the country. Support for the Maidan movement was minimal in the south and east. One public-opinion survey in February 2014 showed that only 20% in the east (including the Donbas) and 8% in the south (including Crimea) sympathised with the Maidan protesters; this figure was 80% in the west and 51% in the centre.[19] The south and east have been increasingly marginalised since the revolution. The Party of Regions, the political machine prevalent there from the late 1990s onward, fell apart after Yanukovych's fall, while the Communist Party of Ukraine, the other major party with support there, was banned by a Kyiv court in September 2015. The annexation of Crimea excluded 2m southerners from the polity, and the Donbas war disenfranchised those in rebel-held territory and also the hundreds of thousands of internally displaced Ukrainians and residents of districts near the line of contact where martial law has been invoked. In the first year of the warfare in the east, most front-line troops were not from regular army units but paramilitary volunteer battalions, some of which had abrasively nationalist leanings; one featured the neo-Nazi Wolfsangel on its banner.[20]

In government-controlled areas of the east and south, popular turnout in the 2014 parliamentary election was signifi-cantly lower than in the west and centre. This helped produce a parliament with a large declaratively pro-Western majority and inclined some to the conclusion that Ukrainians them-selves had profoundly changed their views. It turns out that the quantity of votes cast for such parties was approximately the same as it had been for all previous elections; what had changed was the total number of votes due to low turnout in the south and east.[21] The presence of armed far-right volunteer battalions and their televised public humiliation of candi-dates who had been members of the Party of Regions (some of them dumped unceremoniously into rubbish bins in front of TV cameras) cultivated a climate of fear.[22] Several promi-nent figures associated with the party were murdered in 2015, including an outspoken pro-Russian journalist.

At the time of writing, far-right nationalist figures serve as speaker of the Rada (and thus first in the presidential line of succession) and in senior positions in the interior ministry. The historian who directs the official Institute for National Memory is a nationalist ideologue; he was the author of a 'de-communisation' law that has led to the renaming of thousands of streets, towns, villages and even major cities. Implementation has maximised the law's divisiveness. For example, Moscow Avenue in Kyiv has been renamed Stepan Bandera Avenue in honour of the mid-twentieth-century Ukrainian nationalist who allied with the Nazis against the Red Army. Bandera's name is anathema to millions of Ukrainians, particularly in the south and east of the country, and to many Poles and Jews who associate him with wartime atrocities committed by nationalist groups.

Beyond the empowering of ethno-nationalists, Ukrainians on both sides of the line of contact make a habit of dehumanising one another. To many rebels, the government in Kyiv is a 'fascist junta' and all of its supporters 'Banderites'. In Kyiv, as one Western journalist observed in 2014, empathy has also been notable by its absence:

> Imagine that all the people who opposed your politics for twenty years – all the most backward, poorest, least successful people in the country – got together in one place, declared an independent republic, and *took up arms*? … All the enemies of progress in one place, all the losers and has-beens: wouldn't it be better just to solve the problem once and for all? Wouldn't it be a better long-term solution just to kill as many as you could and scare the shit out of the rest of them, forever? This is what I heard from respectable people in Kiev. Not from the nationalists, but from liberals, from professionals and journalists. All the bad people were in one place – why not kill them all?[23]

Such sentiments are stoked by political leaders, including Poroshenko, who in one statement compared the rebel territories with Mordor, the seat of evil in J.R.R. Tolkien's fantasy novels.[24]

The Ukraine crisis has had a major impact on Russia as well. An economic downturn that began in 2014 has been the longest in its post-Soviet history.[25] After only 0.7% growth in 2014, and a 3.7% drop in 2015, the Russian economy is forecast to contract by 1.2% in 2016. Households have been hit hard; in 2015, real wages decreased by 9.5%.[26] In late 2016 the rouble's exchange rate with the dollar was half what it was in January 2014.

Russia's economic miseries can be traced back to Putin's avoidance of structural reform and the threefold collapse of oil prices in 2014–15. The role of the Ukraine crisis at the margin is thus hard to quantify. One econometric study suggests that Western sanctions cost an average of 2% in quarter-on-quarter drop in GDP between mid-2014 and mid-2015.[27] But the indirect and long-term consequences of the sanctions and the conflict dwarf these direct, short-term ones.[28] Examples include an increase in capital flight that hit the Russian economy's pre-existing weak spot, anaemic levels of investment – the primary threat to long-term growth prospects. Net capital outflows reached approximately 8% of GDP in 2014, before dropping to 3% of GDP in 2015, a relatively normal level for Russia, but still a near-insurmountable challenge to long-term growth. The effective closure of international capital markets to Russian governmental debt prevented the kind of pump-priming used in 2008–09 to stave off a deeper recession. It also forced the authorities to tap reserve funds established during the years of bullish oil prices in order to cover budget shortfalls. The Russian government's long-standing ambition to modernise and diversify the economy away from oil and gas will now be much more difficult to realise because technology transfer from the West via direct investment, co-production and trade has been curtailed. Even if the sanctions are lifted, reputational and political risk will restrain Western firms from returning to the Russian market at pre-crisis levels.

The influence of the Ukraine crisis on Russian domestic politics is every bit as noteworthy. As of the winter of 2013–14, pluralism and democratic institutions were at their lowest ebb since the Soviet collapse. The Maidan Revolution, the annexation of Crimea and the war in the Donbas made a bad situation much worse. The crisis galvanised domestic support for President Putin, sending his approval rating above 80% in March 2014, and keeping it there for 31 months at the time of writing.[29] The Western sanctions, rather than turning Russians against their rulers, educed a defensive reaction, creating the perception of an external threat that the government leveraged to boost popular support.[30] The country's war footing marginalised what remained by way of dissenting voices, since opposition to government policy became akin to treason.

The Kremlin has used the charged political environment to enact legislation that curbs free expression and strictly limits non-governmental links to the West. Examples include stiffer fines for support of separatism and for participating in unauthorised protests; a law requiring any blog with more than 3,000 daily readers to register and be regulated as a media outlet; and a provision allowing the prosecutor's office to brand as 'undesirable' foreign non-governmental organisations that 'threaten constitutional order, defence capabilities or national security'. Once so designated, an organisation is forbidden from maintaining an office in Russia and disseminating its work in the country. By autumn 2016, the US National Endowment for Democracy, the National Democratic Institute, the International Republican Institute and the Open Society Foundation, among others, had been designated undesirable.

As in Ukraine, the conflict also radicalised Russian political discourse. In the months following the seizure of Crimea, TV news anchors, talk-show hosts and pro-government politicians slandered the Kremlin's opponents with the terms 'fifth column' and 'national traitors', terminology that Putin had endorsed in his 18 March 2014 speech announcing the annexation. Politicians and journalists who spoke out online against government policies were hounded by a paid army of pro-government internet trolls.[31] Many other online attacks –

including some that contained threats of violence – came from Russian nationalists who were not on the Kremlin payroll. Nationalist – or more accurately, pan-Slavic neo-imperialist – groups, long frozen out by the authorities, felt newly empowered by the annexation of Crimea and the war in Donbas, in which their members played a role as volunteer fighters.[32]

Russia's position in international politics has also worsened in certain ways since 2014. Its allies in the neighbourhood, while outwardly compliant, worry that one of them might be the next target and hedge against Moscow as much as their circumstances allow. Further west, countries that had previously been on the dovish end of the debate over policy toward Russia within NATO and the EU now see it very differently. In 2013, it would have been inconceivable for the German government to label Russia 'a challenge to the security of our continent', as its 2016 defence white paper did.[33] Berlin has led the effort to maintain unity within the EU on Russia sanctions. Moscow is at serious risk of permanently alienating the entire EU, which as a bloc has long been Russia's largest trading partner and direct investor. With its Western partnerships blighted, Russia is becoming more dependent on China both economically and geopolitically, and over time that may limit its freedom of manoeuvre.

Both Russia and the West have been left worse off by the period of confrontational relations that began in 2014. This Cold War-like climate has impeded cooperation on shared challenges, raised risks of a military clash, and transformed civil conflict into proxy hot wars in Ukraine and Syria. In Europe, new tensions between Russia and NATO have led to a significant deterioration in the security environment. The US withdrew its last battle tank stationed in Europe in 2013; 6,000 had been deployed in Germany at the height of the Cold War. That trend, which facilitated a gigantic peace dividend for the

US and the EU, is now being reversed.[34] The frontier between Russia and the alliance is the locus of a new build-up. The US earmarked US$789m in the fiscal year 2016 and US$3.4bn in 2017 to expand its military presence in East Central Europe, including periodic rotations of armoured and airborne brigades to Poland and the Baltic states. Following consultations at a NATO summit in Warsaw in July 2016, Canada, Germany and the UK now have troops on persistent rotation in the Baltic states. The alliance has also stepped up military rehearsals and manoeuvres, conducting the largest exercise since the end of the Cold War in June 2016.

The NATO moves are a response to genuine threat perceptions of East Central European allies over Russia's behaviour since 2014. Regardless, Moscow sees in them nothing more than a continuation of the long-running process of NATO moving its military infrastructure closer to Russia's borders. In response, Russia has announced a build-up in its Western Military District. In May 2016, Russian Minister of Defence Sergei Shoigu said that the army would form two new infantry divisions in the district by the end of 2016.[35] The Kremlin has also responded asymmetrically. Since 2014, Russia has abducted an Estonian intelligence officer; intensified submarine patrols in the North Atlantic; provided moral and, it has been reported, financial support to eurosceptical and anti-EU parties; and engaged in dangerous brinksmanship in the skies and on the seas, with repeated near misses between Russian air patrols and Western jets (civilian and military) and warships.[36]

NATO and Russia have come closest to a direct military clash in Syria. In September 2015, two days after a meeting between Putin and Obama failed to produce agreement, Moscow began bombing opponents of the Syrian regime – its first military intervention beyond the former Soviet region since the USSR invaded Afghanistan. Russian and NATO warplanes were operating in the same theatre but pursuing competing if not conflicting objectives. Less than three months later, a Turkish pilot downed a Russian military jet near the Syria–Turkey border, the first head-to-head clash between Moscow and a NATO country since the Korean War. Several close calls have occurred in Syria since then, including a near miss between US and Russian warplanes in June 2016.

It bears noting that the shattering of US–Russia ties as a result of the Ukraine crisis helped pave the way for Russia's intervention in Syria. While the facts in and around that war-torn country were the primary motive for the move, it was the breakdown in relations that led Russian decision-makers to believe that only military force could compel Washington to take into account its interests in Syria. And the Ukraine crisis further incentivised Moscow to act in order to break out of the diplomatic isolation that the West had attempted to impose after Crimea and demonstrate that Russia could not be denied its rightful place at the high table of international politics.

The nuclear sabre-rattling associated with the Cold War has returned, although in different forms. In an interview in March 2015, Putin said that he considered putting Russia's nuclear forces on alert during the Crimea operation. In November 2015, Russia's state-owned Channel One displayed images of a general studying plans for a nuclear-armed torpedo, 'Status-6', a doomsday retaliation weapon that could irradiate the entire US east coast. US Secretary of Defense Ashton Carter has named Russia as a top threat to the US and spared the nuclear-weapons budget from any cuts, despite strict budgetary sequestration imposed by Congress.[37] Furthermore, several arms-control and confidence-building regimes that helped end the Cold War peacefully seem near collapse. This is particularly true of the 1987 Intermediate-Range Nuclear Forces Treaty. Russia and the US have accused each other of violating it, and the current atmosphere in the relationship makes a diplomatic resolution almost unthinkable. In short, there is a very real risk of returning to a time when miscalculations in Moscow or Washington can at any moment lead to the destruction of life on earth.

More broadly, this proto-cold war undermines the possibility of collective action to address global challenges. The international order, such as it is, depends on a basic level of comity among the permanent members of the UN Security Council. That level of comity between Russia and the West is gone and will not return for years, if not decades. Constructive interaction within the UN and beyond will thus depend on the ability of governments to compartmentalise, that is, not allowing confrontation on one front to prevent them from cooperating on another. Thus far, the post-2014 record is patchy. Russian and Western diplomats did work together on the 2015 deal to rein in Iran's nuclear programme and on the Paris climate change accord of 2016. However, the tensions have led to the breakdown of cooperation on a range of matters that have nothing to do with Ukraine: Moscow's boycott of the US-led Nuclear Security Summit of March–April 2016 and its renunciation of the Plutonium Management and Disposition Agreement in October 2016, or the suspension of joint counter-terrorism efforts in Afghanistan, to name but a few. Both the US and the Russian governments have been internally divided about the wisdom of compartmentalisation, with those opposed to any cooperation gaining the upper hand as time passes without any prospect of resolving the crisis.

Over and above the billions spent on defence and assistance to Ukraine, the sanctions war has taken an economic toll on the West, though less so than on Russia. One study finds that sanctioning countries had lost US$60.2bn in exports up to June 2015, or about US$3.2bn per month, as a result of the restrictions on trade and financing. The EU has been disproportionately affected, absorbing three-quarters of the loss.[38] Given the parlous state of many eurozone economies, they can ill afford this additional hit; and as a result, the pressure is growing within the EU to roll back the sanctions on the financial and energy sectors that are tethered to Russian implementation of the Minsk II peace plan. If this were to happen despite continuing non-implementation of Minsk II (a not-implausible scenario), major fissures between Washington and Brussels on Russia policy could emerge. Although there is little evidence that sanctions have affected Russian behaviour, they have unquestionably served as an important source of unity between the EU and the US in a crisis that could have easily divided them. A divergence on sanctions would put the current transatlantic consensus on Russia and Ukraine under major strain.

The regional fallout

The Ukraine crisis is thus the paradigmatic example of the negative-sum dynamic in post-Soviet Eurasia. Ukraine, Russia and the Western countries involved are worse off than before. And the contest between Russia and the West over not just Ukraine but all the In-Betweens has only picked up steam. Indeed, Russia and the West have doubled down on the very approach to the region that led to the current stand-off. Across the region, a similar dynamic is playing out: neither the West nor Russia can prevail over the other, while the contest between them is doing damage to the In-Between countries themselves.

Although Euro-Atlantic institutions retain a nominal interest in integrating the In-Betweens, especially Ukraine, Moldova and Georgia, Russia has taken steps that effectively make membership impossible, even if these countries were to meet EU and NATO standards. It has transformed separatist conflicts into geopolitical levers, so that the territorial disputes over

Abkhazia, South Ossetia, Transnistria, Crimea and the Donbas serve as blocks to joining the Western clubs. Although there is no formal rule preventing the EU or NATO from offering membership to states with disputed borders, neither institution wants to import unresolved conflicts that involve Russia. The EU learned its lesson after Cyprus became a member in 2004; the dispute between the Cypriot government and Turkey over Northern Cyprus threw a spanner in Turkey–EU relations and even NATO–EU relations. For NATO, since the Georgia war in 2008 and particularly the conflict in Ukraine, it has become clear that offering collective-security guarantees to countries locked in territorial disputes with Moscow could lead to direct NATO–Russia conflict.

Thus Ukraine, Georgia and Moldova cannot count on restoring their territorial integrity so long as Moscow considers that allowing them to do so would facilitate their membership of Euro-Atlantic institutions. For them, the trade-off is more or less clear: either forgo the aspirations to join the Western clubs or face de facto territorial partition. Putin is reported to have explicitly presented such a swap to Saakashvili before the 2008 war.[39] Most of the time, the trade-off is implicit. The In-Betweens that adhere most closely to Moscow, Armenia and Belarus, are the only two that remain whole. Azerbaijan, the locus of another perennial conflict, is somewhat atypical. Although the clash with Armenia over Nagorno-Karabakh persists, Russia has not stood in the way of a negotiated settlement. Since Baku was never interested in NATO or EU membership or even integration, this exception proves the broader rule that Moscow exploits protracted conflicts in order to gain advantage in the geopolitical and geo-economic competition with the West in the region.

While Russia can effectively prevent the West from winning this competition by preventing resolution of these disputes, it cannot achieve outright victory. By stoking separatist conflicts, it has alienated elites and publics alike in Moldova, Ukraine and Georgia. Its integration offerings remain far less appealing to decision-makers in these countries. Even with its close ally Armenia, Moscow had to coerce Yerevan into EEU membership. Of course, the In-Betweens themselves lose the most from these territorial disputes. Pervasively insecure, these grey zones present numerous challenges, ranging from contraband to human-rights violations.

Along with blocking resolution to festering conflicts, the stepped-up contest between Russia and the West has hamstrung the transition from communist rule in the In-Between countries. These states all suffer, to varying degrees, from a similar set of post-Soviet pathologies: dysfunctional institutions of modern governance; partially reformed economies that lack functioning markets; weak or absent rule of law; 'patronal' politics based on personal connections and dependence rather than ideology or coherent programmes;[40] pervasive corruption; and a close link between political power and control of major financial and industrial assets.[41]

Viewed in comparison with the post-communist countries that joined the EU in 2004 (Poland, the Czech Republic, Hungary, Slovakia, Estonia, Latvia, Lithuania and Slovenia; hereafter, the EU Eight), three of which were Soviet republics, the In-Betweens' disappointing performance after 1991 comes into vivid relief. This can be seen in Figure 1, which shows the 2014 marks for the In-Betweens and a composite score for the EU Eight using measures of governance compiled by the World Bank's Worldwide Governance Indicators project. Figure 2 compares them using Transparency International's 2015 Corruption Perceptions Index. With the partial exception of Georgia, all of the In-Betweens score far lower than the EU Eight on all seven metrics. Figures 3 to 5 indicate the

Figure 1: **Governance**

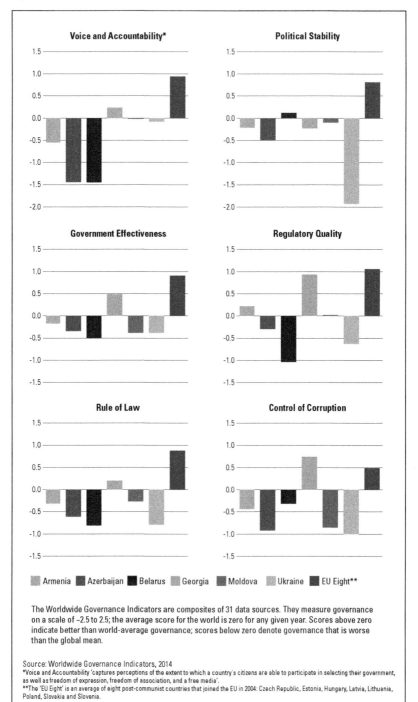

The Worldwide Governance Indicators are composites of 31 data sources. They measure governance on a scale of –2.5 to 2.5; the average score for the world is zero for any given year. Scores above zero indicate better than world-average governance; scores below zero denote governance that is worse than the global mean.

Source: Worldwide Governance Indicators, 2014
*Voice and Accountability 'captures perceptions of the extent to which a country's citizens are able to participate in selecting their government, as well as freedom of expression, freedom of association, and a free media'.
**The 'EU Eight' is an average of eight post-communist countries that joined the EU in 2004: Czech Republic, Estonia, Hungary, Latvia, Lithuania, Poland, Slovakia and Slovenia.

Figure 2: **Corruption perceptions**

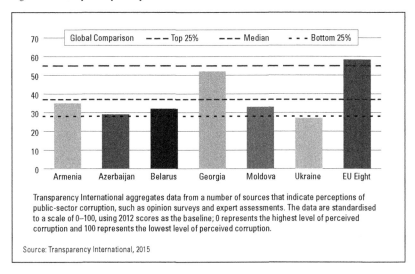

Transparency International aggregates data from a number of sources that indicate perceptions of public-sector corruption, such as opinion surveys and expert assessments. The data are standardised to a scale of 0–100, using 2012 scores as the baseline; 0 represents the highest level of perceived corruption and 100 represents the lowest level of perceived corruption.

Source: Transparency International, 2015

discrepancies in economic governance and democracy since the transition from communist rule began. The European Bank for Reconstruction and Development's competition policy assessment (Figure 5), which measures efforts to reduce abuse of market power and promote a competitive economic environment, gives the In-Betweens and the EU Eight broadly similar marks in the early 1990s. By 2000, there is a significant gap, and it only grows over time. And while Freedom House's political rights and civil liberties scores (Figures 3 and 4) deviate slightly at the start of the transition, that has now become a yawning chasm. Figure 6 demonstrates the meagre economic benefits populations have experienced since the end of central planning. Only Belarus (thanks to generous Russian subsidies) and oil-rich Azerbaijan are significantly better off than they were in the final years of the Soviet Union in terms of GDP per capita. Moldova and Ukraine are poorer today than they were when the transition began. When compared with Poland, Ukraine's underperformance is particularly striking. Ukraine started with a higher GDP per capita, and it is now at less than one-third of Poland's.

Figure 3: **Political rights**

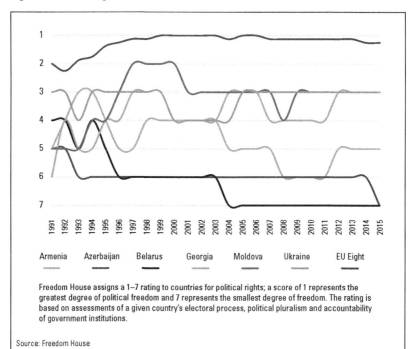

Armenia   Azerbaijan   Belarus   Georgia   Moldova   Ukraine   EU Eight

Freedom House assigns a 1–7 rating to countries for political rights; a score of 1 represents the greatest degree of political freedom and 7 represents the smallest degree of freedom. The rating is based on assessments of a given country's electoral process, political pluralism and accountability of government institutions.

Source: Freedom House

Figure 4: **Civil liberties**

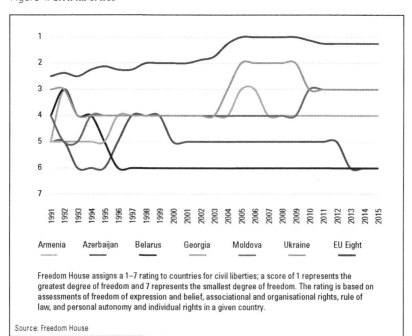

Armenia   Azerbaijan   Belarus   Georgia   Moldova   Ukraine   EU Eight

Freedom House assigns a 1–7 rating to countries for civil liberties; a score of 1 represents the greatest degree of freedom and 7 represents the smallest degree of freedom. The rating is based on assessments of freedom of expression and belief, associational and organisational rights, rule of law, and personal autonomy and individual rights in a given country.

Source: Freedom House

Figure 5: **Competition policy**

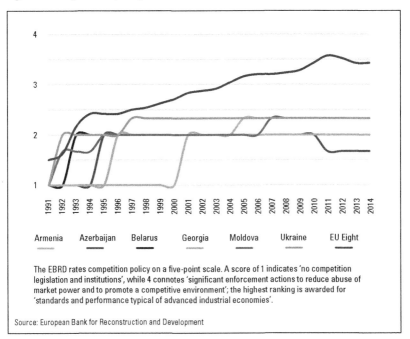

Armenia   Azerbaijan   Belarus   Georgia   Moldova   Ukraine   EU Eight

The EBRD rates competition policy on a five-point scale. A score of 1 indicates 'no competition
legislation and institutions', while 4 connotes 'significant enforcement actions to reduce abuse of
market power and to promote a competitive environment'; the highest ranking is awarded for
'standards and performance typical of advanced industrial economies'.

Source: European Bank for Reconstruction and Development

Figure 6: **GDP per capita**

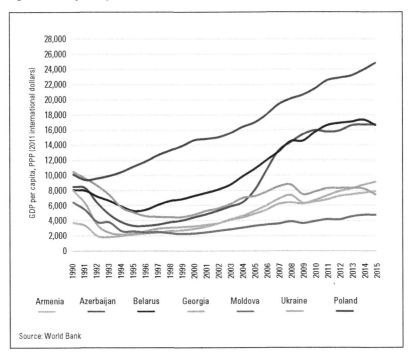

Armenia   Azerbaijan   Belarus   Georgia   Moldova   Ukraine   Poland

Source: World Bank

Many factors contribute to these disparities. The contest between Russia and the West, while by no means the only one, did feed dysfunction in post-Soviet Eurasia in important ways. Firstly, it has helped sustain what Joel Hellman termed a 'partial reform equilibrium' in many of these countries.[42] Hellman noted that the post-communist countries that did not enact sweeping reforms early in the transition had, by the late 1990s, economies that concentrated gains among a small group of 'winners' at a high cost to society as a whole. The winners owed their wealth to the distortions and rents spawned by partial reform, and they used their economic power to 'block further advances in reform that would correct the very distortions on which their initial gains were based'.[43] Hellman's partial reform equilibrium has persisted in all six In-Betweens to the present day. Russian and Western willingness to subsidise political loyalty have played a part. Russia pours money into Belarus through waivers of oil-export tariffs and below-market gas prices; it was willing to demonstrate similar largesse to Ukraine under Yanukovych. The West has also played this game, often in breach of its policy of linking assistance to meaningful reform. Ukraine's current US$17bn IMF programme is its tenth since independence; all previous ones have failed, in the sense that the Fund suspended lending because Kyiv did not implement the required reforms. Within 18 months of signing the current one, the IMF had to amend its by-laws to be able to continue dispensing funds. The notoriously corrupt Moldova would surely have gone bankrupt more than once without its EU lifeline.[44] Following the 2008 war, Washington committed US$1bn in assistance to Georgia, a country of fewer than 5m people. These financial infusions, spurred on by the Russia–West regional contest, made it much easier for governing elites to postpone structural reform indefinitely.

Zero-sum policies on the part of Russia and the Western powers also exacerbated pre-existing political and ethnic cleavages in several of the In-Between states. In Ukraine, as noted earlier, the confrontation has mapped onto, and intensified, internal divisions over identity. Before the crisis, Ukrainians were split down the middle when asked if they would prefer membership of the EU or the Customs Union. The geographic breakdown within Ukraine was stark, with 73% in the western reaches of the country favouring the EU but 62% in the south and 46% in the east favouring the Customs Union in a 2013 poll.[45] After the Crimea annexation and the war in Donbas, the balance shifted somewhat, but regional schisms regarding NATO and EU membership remain.[46]

In Moldova, there are multiple axes of cleavage. Transnistria residents, survey research has consistently revealed, would prefer to become part of Russia than to reunify with Moldova.[47] Even in government-controlled territory on the right bank of the Dniester River, Moldovans are divided; as of October 2015, 45% favour joining the EEU over 38% who prefer the European Union, and the EEU has been gaining ground.[48] The November 2016 election of a president who favours closer ties with the EEU shows the strength of pro-Russian sentiment, although his narrow margin of victory demonstrates the persistent divisions in Moldova's society on these matters. The Gagauz are also far more Russophile than the population as a whole.[49] As in Ukraine, being caught up in the Russia–West battle royal weakens social cohesion and sharpens ethnic and political divides, holding back market reforms and damaging fragile democratic institutions.

In Georgia, there have been similar gradients in opinion between the separatist territories and the rest of the country. Georgians in government-controlled areas are by a long shot the most pro-NATO and pro-EU in post-Soviet Eurasia.[50] South

Ossetia residents are overwhelmingly in favour of becoming part of Russia, and Abkhazians are strongly pro-independence and anti-NATO.[51] Even before the 2008 war, these rifts bedevilled activities to reconcile grievances stemming from the conflicts of the early 1990s. Today, Russia's determination to prevent Tbilisi from restoring control over the breakaway regions prevents any such activities from even getting off the ground. Until the late Soviet period, Georgians and Abkhaz lived in Abkhazia in relative harmony. Following the ethnic cleansing of Georgians from Abkhazia in 1992–93, a full generation of Georgians and Abkhaz have grown up without contact with each other; it is not likely that their children and grandchildren will have any such opportunity.

The geopolitical, geo-economic and geo-ideational tussle that permeates the In-Betweens has also warped party politics and supplanted democratic discourse with demagoguery. In Moldova and Ukraine, parties and leaders have declared themselves pro-Western to capitalise on popular desire for good government, which many citizens associate with the West. When in power, however, they all too often have proven to be as corrupt and incompetent as their so-called pro-Russian opponents.

Additionally, the contest for influence between Russia and the West has hobbled US and EU efforts to further reform in post-Soviet Eurasia. This is partly a function of practicalities: when geopolitical, geo-economic and geo-ideational issues are at the top of the agenda, other problems fall by the wayside. But at times when the contest is particularly intense, Western policymakers have deliberately downplayed human rights and democracy-related problems for fear of pushing countries into Russia's embrace. EU backpedalling on conditionality with Yanukovych is one example discussed earlier. The tepid Western reaction to the crackdown on protesters in Tbilisi in

November 2007 is another. As Human Rights Watch noted in its report on the incident,

> Georgia has been seen as a small but crucial bulwark to counter Russian dominance in the region and as an important ally for the United States. It has also been held up as an example of a successful transition to democracy in the former Soviet Union region. As a result, the US and EU have refrained from criticizing Saakashvili in public and from engaging in robust discussion of the country's human rights problems.[52]

Since the Ukraine crisis, this problem has become more acute. As Nelli Babayan notes, 'the bargaining power of some [regional states] vis-à-vis the West seems to have increased, although their compliance with the rules and norms promoted by the West [has] not meaningfully changed or [has] in some cases even decreased'.[53] Belarus is a case in point. In February 2016 the EU rolled back sanctions on President Lukashenko and his coterie as well as several state-controlled firms. EU officials will admit that in doing so they ignored Minsk's non-compliance with Brussels' stated requirements regarding human rights, on the reasoning that Belarus had become a 'battleground of powers'.[54] The US gladly joined the EU effort to placate a man former secretary of state Condoleezza Rice had once called 'the last dictator in Europe'. In March 2016 a senior Pentagon official travelled to Minsk to meet with Lukashenko and restart a military-to-military relationship that had been on ice for nearly a decade.

All of this saps the West's ability to push the region's governments to reform. Soft-pedalling criticism of rulers who pledge fealty also feeds a widespread belief that public censure regarding human rights, democracy or reform is merely an instrument to punish disloyalty. Inconsistency in airing such critiques across countries or over time in particular countries undercuts those officials who do speak out about abuses or push their interlocutors to reform. It is easier for the latter to brush off such concerns if they receive mixed messages or can point to double standards. By treating the In-Betweens as spoils to be won, the West also gives all the region's leaders a foil against almost any expression of disapproval: the threat of turning to Moscow. In the case of Ukraine post-2014, where such a threat is no longer credible, Western states have been reluctant to withhold public statements of support and financial assistance on the logic that the country cannot be allowed to fail. It is almost as if Ukraine's rulers are holding their own country hostage and extorting ransom.[55]

Moving past the negative-sum game

The Cold War was brought to a peaceful conclusion by statesmen impelled by a sense of urgency, a feeling that they were 'running against a clock' and that the window of opportunity for decisive action might soon close. The regnant mood in the current crisis is one of resolve to maintain entrenched positions, not urgency about finding a solution. The frozen conflicts of post-Soviet Eurasia, up in number with the addition of Crimea and the Donbas, are mirrored in policymakers' frozen thinking. Even a well-meaning OSCE Panel of Eminent Persons on European Security as a Common Project, commissioned in December 2014, came up with little that was new. The final report of the panel mostly rehearsed well-known Western and Russian narratives of the post-Soviet period.[56]

This historical moment is different from that of a generation ago. There is something to be said for caution, honouring the 'Do no harm' principle. But in this case caution has with time settled into stale and unreflective policies. It is high time to revive the debate over the future of post-Soviet Eurasia; to reconnect it with realities on the ground; and to move past summations of the problem, and of the misbehaviour of this or that side, to innovative and realistic proposals for moving past the negative-sum game.

Contestation over the region began unplanned, and remained a low-key affair for more than a decade after the end of the Cold War. With the passage of time, the main external actors became more purposive and disciplined in seeking unilateral advantage. Rather than developing the habit of cooperating to mutual benefit, they regularly aimed for wins at the other's expense. Instinctual counter-escalation occurred in response, as governments doubled down on their policies, even when those policies were ill-considered and counterproductive. The regional players became less capable of playing the game with nuance, mostly because the outside powers were more likely than before to demand fully fledged commitment to their point of view.[57] All in all, zero-sum approaches to geopolitics, geo-economics and geo-ideas stood in the way of mutual accommodation. In turn, they also produced negative-sum results. State boundaries have been redrawn and animosities and even hatreds aroused, while relations among global powers are in tatters.

The *sine qua non* for a reassessment must be an acknowledgement that both Russian and Western policies toward post-Soviet Eurasia have reached a dead end. For Russia, that means recognition that the zero-sum approach to its neighbourhood has been costly in the extreme, risky and self-defeating. The recurrent resort to coercion, be it political, military or economic, has alienated countries that might otherwise have naturally been drawn to Russia. The US and the EU must acknowledge that, despite success in East Central Europe, further application of the solution of the 1990s – the extension of Euro-Atlantic institutions eastward toward the Russian border, but not across it – is no longer viable. This prefab paradigm, mechanical growth of pre-existing institutions without negotiating terms among all affected parties, including Russia, and without compromises, is now unworkable. Continuing with the status quo will perpetuate instability and poor governance in the states of the region and a long-term Cold War-like atmosphere in West–Russia relations. The Ukraine crisis that has been with us since 2014 amply demonstrates this reality.

One of the ironies of recent frictions is that at this juncture neither NATO nor the EU is in a position to offer full-scale membership to any of the In-Betweens. This would be the case even if there were no frozen conflicts in the region, and even if the In-Betweens met the standards of good governance, functioning markets and democratic practices required for either EU or NATO membership. NATO member states are at odds on extending security guarantees to countries that Russia habitually threatens and sometimes invades. The EU is in the deepest crisis of its existence, given the eurozone mess, economic torpor, unruly waves of migration from the Middle East and North Africa, terrorism and Brexit. With its survival in question, adding new members is not a priority.

Recognising the reality that the policy of institutional enlarge- ment in post-communist Europe and Eurasia, its past successes aside, has run its course does not mean that the West must accept Russian domination of its neighbours. In fact, the further enlarge- ment of Russia-led institutions in the region is not a plausible solution either, regardless of what policy the West adopts. Those already in the Russian institutional fold remain there either under duress or for lack of better options; most would likely run for the exits if they could.[58] There is little support anywhere else for the Russian blueprint for regional governance.

Western and Russian policymakers would also be well advised to rethink the geo-ideas that often underpin their policies. It is not tenable for the West to insist on the right of all countries to make their own choices while at the same time being unable or unwilling to grant them those choices (like NATO and EU membership) or to take responsibility for the consequences of choosing. The EU is poorly served by the pious assertion of normative hegemony – the inherent superiority of its systems and structures – in an area where that hegemony is contested, both by Russia and by the reform-allergic systems of the In-Betweens.[59] Russia's concept of indivisible security often boils down to a yearning for an accord among great powers, Yalta-style, that would reinforce rather than remove divisions in the region. Such a deal would not work even if it were agreed to, which it will not be. The Kremlin's *idée fixe* that Russia needs to be the leader of a pack of post-Soviet states in order to be taken seriously as a global power broker is more a feel-good mantra than a fact-based strategy, and it irks even the closest of allies.

The towel should also be thrown in on the geo-ideational shadow-boxing over the Russian assertion of a sphere of influence in post-Soviet Eurasia and the Western opposition to it. Would either side be able to specify what precisely they mean by a regional sphere of influence? How would it differ from, say, US relations with western-hemisphere states, or from Germany's with its EU neighbours? Clearly there are differences, but they are rarely specified. Is it realistic to think that Russia, an order of magnitude weightier than the states at its doorstep, would have *no* influence over them? And is it reasonable to expect any country of Russia's global significance to observe from the wings as geo-economic and geopolitical blocs closed to it gradually absorb many of the countries on its borders? As Charles Kupchan, who has served as the Obama administration's senior National Security Council official for the In-Betweens, once wrote, 'The United States would hardly sit by idly if Russia formed an alliance with Mexico and Canada and started building military installations along the US border.'[60]

Russia's insistence that the In-Betweens and the Central Asians constitute its sphere of influence, or its zone of 'privileged interests' as Dmitry Medvedev put it, is as devoid of meaning as the fervent Western refutation of it. What exactly are privileged interests? Is the privilege asserted absolute, relative or at the margin? Is Russia truly claiming that it alone will have final say in the area, and would its writ be only over national security or also over domestic government, social policy and so forth? Are the ways the Kremlin chooses to exercise its influence not as important as the fact of influence itself? What would Moscow presume to do about the preferences of the states in this 'sphere', and especially those that have since 1991 sought alternative partnerships to balance against the regional hegemon? Even if Western leaders were to shed their qualms and seek a grand bargain with Russia, can any deal that might result really function if it does not take these countries' views into account?

Breaking the taboo on open-ended, precondition-free dialogue on the regional order is the essential first step if we are to mitigate the ruinous geopolitical, geo-economic and geo-ideational competition and end the Russia–West confrontation that has reached such dangerous levels in recent years. For the West, allowing the ghosts of Yalta to stand in the way of such a conversation with Russia is negligent and in the final analysis self-defeating. For Moscow, it is untenable to expect that its neighbours can be forever excluded from a dialogue that will have direct implications for them.

Holding such talks in the current atmosphere of mistrust, mutual recrimination and fear-mongering will require a significant investment of political capital. And the process of moving beyond current adversarial approaches to the region and finding common ground will take time. For this process to succeed, all parties would also have to scale back their maximalist objectives and be prepared for compromises that will leave no one fully satisfied. The West needs to cease holding out for Russia to surrender and accept its terms. Russia must stop pining for the good old days of great-power politics, be it the Big Three of 1945 or the Concert of Europe of 1815–1914, and accept that its neighbours will have to have a say in any agreement that affects them. The neighbours should stop seeking national salvation from without, and recognise that it will be up to them, first and foremost, to bring about their countries' security and well-being.

If such talks ever take place, they could consider new institutional arrangements for the In-Betweens that would serve as a bridge between the Euro-Atlantic institutions and their Russia-led counterparts.[61] Such an agreement would go a long way toward moving past the negative-sum game by both diminishing great-power rivalry in the region and alleviating some of the challenges faced by the In-Betweens. The following is a preliminary list of criteria the new arrangements would have to meet in order to do so:

- They must be acceptable to all concerned parties.
- Priority should be given for the foreseeable future to economic growth, reform and modernisation in the In-Between countries. The states in question should be allowed to pursue ties with both the EU and the EEU as they see fit, permitting multi-directional integration rather than insisting on obligations that make it impossible.
- Parties to the negotiations should pledge to seek mutual agreement before pursuing any change to the region's institutional architecture, and should commit to regular,

inclusive consultations. This would rule out attempts to make unilateral changes to the status quo.

- All parties must recommit to respect each other's sovereignty and territorial integrity, and to refrain from the use of force in dispute resolution. As part of this process, Russia would commit to withdraw its military from areas where sovereignty is not disputed by any party, such as Transnistria and the Donbas, in the fullness of time.

- Rather than make the negotiations contingent on resolution of territorial disputes, the arrangements themselves should create status-neutral humanitarian, security and economic measures in and around the conflict zones. The parties would provide for a guarantee of status neutrality – explicitly putting the core political disputes on the back-burner – so that these measures can be negotiated and implemented without crossing any state's red lines. Countries with irreconcilable positions would be able to address practical issues affecting inhabitants of the frozen-conflict zones without ceding their positions. Such steps would at a minimum ease tensions and human suffering and might lay the foundation for a political settlement.

Even if these broad criteria are satisfied, a great deal of tough negotiating would be unavoidable. It goes without saying that doing so under the current circumstances will be extremely difficult. But it is not impossible. The Helsinki Final Act, perhaps an even more ambitious undertaking, was hammered out in the mid-1970s, at the height of Cold War tensions.[62] Just as that document did not in itself end the Cold War, the negotiation we are foreseeing, even if it succeeds, could help to alleviate tensions but would not eliminate them completely. And with the In-Betweens present at the table, the ghosts of Yalta would not be awakened.

A necessary first step is for the West to seek explicitly a compromise along these lines as a matter of policy. Russia is unlikely to take this first step, in part because many in Moscow still feel spurned after Medvedev's attempt in 2008–09. But it is worthwhile testing the proposition that Russia would respond positively to an offer of talks.

Taking that first step does not require the West to bow to Russian demands. The proposed bargain would require all parties to make painful compromises. The West would have to acknowledge that the model that worked so well in East Central Europe is not going to work for post-Soviet Eurasia. Russia would have to strictly adhere to the limits the new arrangements would impose on its influence and to forswear further military encroachment on its neighbours. At a more basic level, Moscow would have to accept that its neighbours are well and truly sovereign states and that they have to be treated as such, even when it is inconvenient to do so.

Fruitful talks on this set of issues are not just a way to create a modicum of great-power comity. Negotiating new institutional mechanisms for the regional architecture in post-Soviet Eurasia would give the countries of the region a more decent chance than they have had – discounting all the soaring oratory – at security, reform and prosperity. Pursuing the status quo of unbridled contestation is a recipe for continued insecurity, political dysfunction and economic backwardness within the region. We will see repetitions of ruinous scenes like the destruction of Donetsk's Sergei Prokofiev International Airport, and maybe worse.

The uncomfortable truth is that today neither Russia nor the West believes that the other would be willing to accept a compromise. Those who rule Russia are convinced that the West will forever push to extend its reach right up to Russia's borders, and even inside them. Many Western policymakers are convinced that Russia for its part is a predator state, absolutely committed to domination of its neighbours.

Sadly, neither of these threat perceptions is completely baseless. Those who hold them can rightly point to numerous reasons why the talks we propose might fail. But the frightening consequences of a lengthy confrontation more than justify an attempt to find agreement. Not making such an attempt – and thus ensuring a new cold war – would be the height of policy negligence. One cold war was enough.

NOTES

Introduction

1 Prokofiev's music was considered 'formalist' by Communist Party ideologists. For this reason and because of his long period of exile, he did his work as something of a pariah, but he was never arrested or harmed. In a striking coincidence, Prokofiev died on the same day (5 March 1953) as the Soviet dictator Joseph Stalin.

2 One of many eye-opening video presentations of the cyborgs' activity may be found at https://www.youtube.com/watch?v=3Pf3HjUwtWU&feature=youtu.be.

3 We are aware that up to a point gains and losses are in the eye of the beholder, that in the real world they may come in mixed packages, and that even individuals who agree on objectives and strategy may disagree about the success or failure of actions they have taken collectively. Throughout this book, we do our best to make detached and objective assessments of gains and losses, while acknowledging that others, particularly those directly involved in the process, might use different metrics.

4 Parsing through the various explanations is complicated by the wide range of justifications put forth by the participants themselves, particularly the leaders of Russia.

5 Serhy Yekelchyk, *The Conflict in Ukraine: What Everyone Needs to Know* (Oxford: Oxford University Press, 2015), p. 4.

6 Andrew Wilson, *Ukraine Crisis: What It Means for the West* (New Haven, CT: Yale University Press, 2014), p. vii.

7 John Mearsheimer, 'Why the Ukraine Crisis Is the West's Fault', *Foreign Affairs*, vol. 93, no. 5, September/October 2014, pp. 82, 84.

8 Andrei Tsygankov, 'Vladimir Putin's Last Stand: the Sources of Russia's Ukraine Policy', *Post-Soviet Affairs*, vol. 31, no. 4, July 2015, p. 280.

9 Richard Sakwa, *Frontline Ukraine: Crisis in the Borderlands* (London: I.B. Tauris, 2015), p. 255.

10 Kathryn Stoner and Michael McFaul, 'Who Lost Russia (This Time)? Vladimir Putin', *Washington Quarterly*, vol. 38, no. 2, Summer 2015, p. 175.

11 *Ibid.*, p. 181.

12 Rajan Menon and Eugene Rumer, *Conflict in Ukraine: The Unwinding of the Post-Cold War Order* (Cambridge, MA: MIT Press, 2015), pp. xix, 162.

Chapter One

1   Phrase taken from the foundational argument about geo-economics in Edward N. Luttwak, 'From Geopolitics to Geo-Economics: Logic of Conflict, Grammar of Commerce', *National Interest*, no. 20, Summer 1990, pp. 17–23.

2   Lest this triad sound overly rationalistic, we concede that non-rational variables – such as arrogance, bureaucratic red tape, carelessness and sloth – also entered into the picture we describe. We are grateful to Neil MacFarlane for drawing our attention to this point. Our take, though, is that these factors were at work on all sides and did not tip the outcome in any one direction.

3   'Text of Havel's Speech to Congress', 22 February 1990, https://www.washingtonpost.com/archive/politics/1990/02/22/text-of-havels-speech-to-congress/df98e177-778e-4c26-bd96-980089c4fcb2/.

4   James Baker, *The Politics of Diplomacy: Revolution, War and Peace, 1989–1992* (New York: G.P. Putnam's Sons, 1995), p. 158.

5   *Ibid.*, p. 247.

6   George H.W. Bush and Brent Scowcroft, *A World Transformed* (New York: Knopf, 1998), pp. 205–6.

7   Gorbachev quoted in Milan Svec, 'The Prague Spring: 20 Years Later', *Foreign Affairs*, vol. 55, no. 5, Summer 1988, pp. 981–1001.

8   Mary Elise Sarotte, *1989: The Struggle to Create Post-Cold War Europe* (Princeton, NJ: Princeton University Press, 2009), p. 91. Interestingly this heroic multinationalism, as Sarotte tags it, was also the dream of the socialist dissidents who helped bring down East German Communism, and of liberal oppositionists in Poland and Czechoslovakia.

9   Within the Western alliance, Margaret Thatcher's British government and, less so, François Mitterrand's government in Paris had reservations about reunification but went along with it.

10 The sequence in which this was done was quite complex. For the details, see Mary Elise Sarotte, 'Not One Inch Eastward? Bush, Baker, Kohl, Genscher, Gorbachev, and the Origin of Russian Resentment Toward NATO Enlargement in February 1990', *Diplomatic History*, vol. 34, no. 1, January 2010, pp. 119–40.

11 Gorbachev ran the proposition of the Soviet Union joining NATO by George Bush later that month and in July, this time severing it from German unification. See Sarotte, *1989*, chap. 5; Baker, *The Politics of Diplomacy*, pp. 251–2; Philip Zelikow and Condoleezza Rice, *Germany Unified and Europe Transformed: A Study in Statecraft* (Cambridge, MA: Harvard University Press, 1995), p. 280; James Baker, 'Russia in NATO?', *Washington Quarterly*, vol. 25, no. 1, Winter 2002, p. 102.

12 Bush and Scowcroft, *A World Transformed*, pp. 300–1.

13 'Charter of Paris for a New Europe', 1990, http://www.osce.org/mc/39516?download=true.

14 Baker, *The Politics of Diplomacy*, pp. 173, 196.

15 Bill Keller, 'Gorbachev, in Finland, Disavows Any Right of Regional Intervention', *New York Times*, 26 October 1989, http://www.nytimes.com/1989/10/26/world/gorbachev-

in-finland-disavows-any-right-of-regional-intervention.html.

16 Gorbachev and Kissinger quoted in Bennett Kovrig, *Of Walls and Bridges: The United States & Eastern Europe* (New York: New York University Press, 1991), p. 360.

17 Stephen Kux, 'Neutrality and New Thinking', in Roger E. Kanet, Deborah Nutter Miner and Tamara J. Resler (eds), *Soviet Foreign Policy in Transition* (Cambridge: Cambridge University Press, 1992), pp. 110–13. The papers in this collection were written for an academic conference in 1990. By the time they came out, there was of course no such thing as Soviet foreign policy.

18 The treaty restoring Austria, under occupation since 1945, as a sovereign state was signed by the Allied powers and the Austrian government in May 1955. The Soviets made it a condition of signing that neutrality be written into the constitution, which was done by act of parliament five months later. Kissinger specifically suggested an Austrian-type arrangement for Czechoslovakia, Hungary and Poland. See Gerald B.H. Solomon, *The NATO Enlargement Debate, 1990–1997: Blessings of Liberty* (Washington DC: Center for Strategic and International Studies, 1998), p. 8. For broader discussion, see Richard Ned Lebow, 'Understanding Change in International Politics: The Soviet Empire's Demise and the International System', in Richard Ned Lebow and Thomas Risse-Kappen (eds), *International Relations Theory and the End of the Cold War* (New York: Columbia University Press, 1995), pp. 155–6.

19 Joshua R. Itzkowitz Shifrinson, 'Deal or No Deal? The End of the Cold War and the U.S. Offer to Limit NATO Expansion', *International Security*, vol. 40, no. 4, Spring 2016, pp. 7–44; Baker quotation at p. 30. A well-argued alternative interpretation is Mark Kramer, 'The Myth of a No-NATO-Enlargement Pledge to Russia', *Washington Quarterly*, vol. 32, no. 2, April 2009, pp. 39–61.

20 'It was definitely a violation of the spirit of the statements and assurances made to us in 1990.' Maxim Korshunov, 'Mikhail Gorbachev: I Am against All Walls', Russia Beyond the Headlines, 16 October 2014, http://rbth.com/international/2014/10/16/mikhail_gorbachev_i_am_against_all_walls_40673.html.

21 Shifrinson, 'Deal or No Deal?', p. 40. Shifrinson also documents (p. 38) that some working-level officials in the Department of State and Pentagon penned briefs as soon as October 1990 about the desirability of keeping NATO's door ajar and 'not [giving] the East Europeans the impression that NATO is forever a closed club'.

22 Sarotte, *1989*, p. 200.

23 *Ibid.*, pp. 200–1.

24 Mary Elise Sarotte, 'A Broken Promise? What the West Really Told Moscow about NATO Expansion', *Foreign Affairs*, vol. 93, no. 5, September/October 2014, p. 97. Sarotte has written that this was done 'by design'. We agree that one effect of the institutional design adopted at the time was to place Russia on Europe's periphery, but we do not see this as the intended result.

25 Along with Russia, Armenia, Azerbaijan, Kazakhstan, Kyrgyzstan, Moldova, Tajikistan, Turkmenistan and Uzbekistan were founding members. Georgia did not join until 1993.

26 The three Baltic states had been independent countries between the

world wars. The United States had never recognised their annexation by the Soviet Union in 1940.

[27] Belarus and Ukraine had formally been members of the UN since 1945, despite their subordination to the Soviet government in Moscow.

[28] Strobe Talbott, *Russia Hand: A Memoir of Presidential Diplomacy* (New York: Random House, 2002), p. 94.

[29] *Ibid.*

[30] The report was published in 'Perspektivy rasshireniya NATO i interesy Rossii: Doklad Sluzhby vneshnei razvedki', *Izvestiya*, 25 November 1993. For a summary, see Steven Erlanger, 'Russia Warns NATO on Expanding East', *New York Times*, 26 November 1993.

[31] For the September letter, see Roger Cohen, 'Yeltsin Opposes Expansion of NATO in Eastern Europe', *New York Times*, 2 October 1993, http://www.nytimes.com/1993/10/02/world/yeltsin-opposes-expansion-of-nato-in-eastern-europe.html.

[32] 'Interv'yu c ministrom inostrannykh del Rossiiskoi Federatsii Andreem Kozyrevem', *Rossiiskaya gazeta*, 7 December 1993.

[33] Quotations from a declassified memo of the conversation at 'Secretary Christopher's Meeting with President Yeltsin, 10/22/93, Moscow', http://cdn.warontherocks.com/wp-content/uploads/2016/07/Christopher-Yeltsin-1993-MemCon.pdf. See the discussion in James Goldgeier, 'Promises Made, Promises Broken? What Yeltsin Was Told About NATO in 1993 and Why It Matters', War on the Rocks, 12 July 2016, http://warontherocks.com/2016/07/promises-made-promises-broken-what-yeltsin-was-told-about-nato-in-1993-and-why-it-matters/.

[34] 'The President's News Conference With Visegrad Leaders in Prague', 12 January 1994, http://www.presidency.ucsb.edu/ws/?pid=49832.

[35] James M. Goldgeier, *Not Whether But When: The U.S. Decision to Enlarge NATO* (Washington DC: Brookings Institution Press, 1999), p. 20.

[36] Stephen Sestanovich, 'Could It Have Been Otherwise?', *American Interest*, vol. 10, no. 5, 2015, http://www.the-american-interest.com/2015/04/14/could-it-have-been-otherwise/.

[37] Goldgeier, *Not Whether But When*, pp. 169–70. Exhaustive accounts of the domestic politics of NATO enlargement (and the roles of politicians, business interests, think tanks and ethnic lobbies) can be found in these books: Ronald D. Asmus, *Opening NATO's Door: How the Alliance Remade Itself for a New Era* (New York: Council on Foreign Relations, 2002); George W. Grayson, *Strange Bedfellows: NATO Marches East* (Lanham, MD: University Press of America, 1999).

[38] Quotations from Asmus, *Opening NATO's Door*, p. 192; Evgenii Primakov, *Vstrechi na perekrestkakh* (Moscow: Tsentrpoligraf, 2015), pp. 221–2.

[39] Daniel Deudney and G. John Ikenberry, 'The Unravelling of the Cold War Settlement', *Survival: Global Politics and Strategy*, vol. 51, no. 6, December 2009–January 2010, p. 51.

[40] See the summary in Maksim Yusin, 'Moskve ne udalos' provesti perestroiku SBSE', *Izvestiya*, 12 October 1994.

[41] Primakov, *Vstrechi na perekrestkakh*, p. 221.

[42] 'Founding Act on Mutual Relations, Cooperation and Security between NATO and the Russian Federation

Signed in Paris, France', 27 May 1997, http://www.nato.int/cps/en/natohq/official_texts_25468.htm.

43 Hiski Haukkala, 'Russian Reactions to the European Neighborhood Policy', *Problems of Post-Communism*, vol. 55, no. 5, September 2008, pp. 40–8.

44 Sestanovich, 'Could It Have Been Otherwise?'

45 Critics also brought up the central role of Russia and Boris Yeltsin in dismantling the Soviet regime. George F. Kennan in 1998 declared that expansion of the Alliance over Russia's objections was 'turning our backs on the very people who mounted the greatest bloodless revolution in history to remove that Soviet regime'. Quoted in Thomas L. Friedman, 'Foreign Affairs; Now a Word from X', *New York Times*, 2 May 1998.

46 The comment by Goldgeier in 1999 sums up this miscalculation: 'Once the NATO–Russia Founding Act was signed … it was difficult for critics to make the case that Russia found enlargement unacceptable.' Goldgeier, *Not Whether But When*, p. 172.

47 See Milada Anna Vachudova, *Europe Undivided: Democracy, Leverage, and Integration After Communism* (Oxford: Oxford University Press, 2005).

48 For more on the role of external powers here, see Alexander Cooley, *Great Games, Local Rules: The New Great Power Contest in Central Asia* (Oxford: Oxford University Press, 2012).

49 In the European Union, for example, the French, British and Italian economies are roughly two-thirds the size of the German. In East Asia, China and Japan are about equal in economic strength. In the Western Hemisphere, the US economy, in current prices, is about seven times the size of the

Brazilian economy and nine times the size of the Canadian.

50 David A. Lake, 'The Rise, Fall, and Future of the Russian Empire: A Theoretical Interpretation', in Karen Dawisha and Bruce Parrott (eds), *The End of Empire? The Transformation of the USSR in Comparative Perspective* (Armonk, NY: M.E. Sharpe, 1997), pp. 54, 55.

51 Nunn–Lugar funds were also used to dispose of chemical and biological weapons. Russia participated in the programme until 2015. The negotiations with the Ukrainians are described in Graham Allison, 'What Happened to the Soviet Superpower's Nuclear Arsenal?', Discussion Paper 2012, Belfer Center for Science and International Affairs, John F. Kennedy School of Government, Harvard University, March 2012, http://belfercenter.ksg.harvard.edu/files/3%2014%2012%20Final%20What%20Happened%20to%20Soviet%20Arsenals.pdf.

52 From the full text in Russian at 'Strategicheskii kurs Rossii s gosudarstvami – uchastnikami Sodruzhestva Nezavisimykh Gosudarstv', 14 September 1995, http://www.mid.ru/foreign_policy/official_documents/-/asset_publisher/CptICkB6BZ29/content/id/427752 (italics added). President Putin in 2005 nullified two minor articles of the decree, leaving the rest of it intact.

53 Quoted in Talbott, *Russia Hand*, p. 80.

54 Yevgeny Ambartsumov, quoted in Emil Pain, 'Mezhnatsional'nye konflikty v politicheskoi igre', *Nezavisimaya gazeta*, 10 July 1992.

55 Quoted in 'Chto bylo na nedele', *Kommersant*, 6 March 1993.

56 For an early assessment, see Fiona

Hill and Pamela Jewett, '"Back in the USSR": Russia's Intervention in the Internal Affairs of the Former Soviet Republics and the Implications for United States Policy Toward Russia', Strengthening Democratic Institutions Project, John F. Kennedy School of Government, Harvard University, January 1994, http://belfercenter.hks. harvard.edu/files/Back%20in%20 the%20USSR%201994.pdf.

57 Christoph Zürcher, *The Post-Soviet Wars: Rebellion, Ethnic Conflict, and Nationhood in the Caucasus* (New York: New York University Press, 2007), p. 141.

58 'Remarks in a Town Meeting with Russian Citizens in Moscow', 14 January 1994, https://www.gpo.gov/ fdsys/pkg/WCPD-1994-01-24/pdf/ WCPD-1994-01-24-Pg67.pdf.

59 For details on activities in Transnistria, see Rebecca Chamberlain-Creanga and Lyndon K. Allin, 'Acquiring Assets, Debts, and Citizens: Russia and the Micro-Foundations of Transnistria's Stalemated Conflict', *Demokratizatsiya: The Journal of Post-Soviet Democratization*, vol. 18, no. 4, Fall 2010, pp. 329–56.

60 Daniel W. Drezner, *The Sanctions Paradox: Economic Statecraft and International Relations* (Cambridge: Cambridge University Press, 1999), pp. 131–248. See also Margarita Balmaceda, 'Gas, Oil, and Linkages between Domestic and Foreign Policies: The Case of Ukraine', *Europe–Asia Studies*, vol. 50, no. 2, March 1998, pp. 257–86; Tor Bukkvoll, 'Off the Cuff Politics—Explaining Russia's Lack of a Ukraine Strategy', *Europe–Asia Studies*, vol. 53, no. 8, December 2001, pp. 1141–57; Margarita Balmaceda, *Politics of Energy Dependency: Ukraine,* *Belarus, and Lithuania Between Domestic Oligarchs and Russian Pressure* (Toronto: University of Toronto Press, 2013).

61 John P. Willerton and Mikhail A. Beznosov, 'Russia's Pursuit of Its Eurasian Security Interests: Weighing the CIS and Alternative Bilateral–Muiltilateral Arrangemnets', in Katlijn Malfliet, Lien Verpoest and Evgeny Vinokurov (eds), *The CIS, the EU and Russia: The Challenges of Integration* (Basingstoke: Palgrave Macmillan, 2007), p. 50.

62 Taras Kuzio, 'Geopolitical Pluralism in the CIS: The emergence of GUUAM', *European Security*, vol. 9, no. 2, Summer 2000, p. 84.

63 Russia and Belarus further muddied the picture by forming a mostly fictional 'union state' in 1997.

64 The Ukrainians inserted a clause into the 2003 agreement specifying that the new entity was not to act contrary to their constitution or to the objective of fostering integration with the European Union.

65 Uzbekistan, an original party to the treaty (which was signed in its capital city), withdrew from it in 1999, as did Azerbaijan and Georgia, which had joined in 1993. Uzbekistan was to rejoin in 2006, only to pull out again in 2012.

66 Martha Brill Olcott, Anders Aslund and Sherman W. Garnett, *Getting It Wrong: Regional Cooperation and the Commonwealth of Independent States* (Washington DC: Carnegie Endowment for International Peace, 1999), pp. 95–6.

67 The eight working groups, for example, largely limited themselves to one annual meeting each, often on the margins of larger gatherings. A number of agreements were never

implemented, and others went into effect in only one or several of the member states. Details on the GUAM organisation can be found at http://guam-organization.org/ and more lucidly at a site maintained by one of the GUAM principals, Moldova: http://www.mfa.gov.md/about-guam-en/.

68 Olcott, Aslund and Garnett, *Getting It Wrong*, p. 208.

69 Jakob Tolstrup, *Russia vs. the EU: The Competition for Influence in Post-Soviet States* (Boulder, CO: Lynne Rienner, 2013), p. 130.

70 Authors' interview with a former senior Russian official, December 2015.

71 For Brzezinski's initial statement to this effect, see Zbigniew Brzezinski, 'The Premature Partnership', *Foreign Affairs*, vol. 73, no. 2, March–April 1994, pp. 67–82.

72 Warren Christopher, 'NATO PLUS', *Washington Post*, 9 January 1994, https://www.washingtonpost.com/archive/opinions/1994/01/09/nato-plus/88b3d1a6-8111-4491-bbf0-e6267b0dae95/?utm_term=.0fe94b86f2ed.

73 William H. Hill, *Russia, the Near Abroad, and the West: Lessons from the Moldova–Transdniestria Conflict* (Washington DC: Woodrow Wilson Center Press, 2012), p. 36.

74 Ronald Asmus of the RAND Corporation, who would shortly join the Clinton administration, wrote with two fellow enlargement advocates in 1995 that for the time being, 'The West would prefer to have a Finlandised Ukraine – politically and economically stable and pro-Western, but militarily neutral'. Ronald D. Asmus, Richard L. Kugler and F. Stephen Larrabee, 'NATO Expansion: The Next Steps', *Survival: Global Politics and Strategy*, vol. 37, no. 1, Spring 1995, pp. 7–33.

75 Primakov, *Vstrechi na perekrestkakh*, p. 371.

76 Steve LeVine, *The Oil and the Glory: The Pursuit of Empire and Fortune on the Caspian Sea* (New York: Random House, 2007), p. 215.

77 *Ibid.*, p. 221. Russian calculations are well laid out in Douglas W. Blum, 'The Russian–Georgian Crisis and Baku–Tbilisi–Ceyhan', PONARS Policy Memo, no. 252, October 2002, http://www.ponarseurasia.org/sites/default/files/policy-memos-pdf/pm_0252.pdf.

78 Mark Kramer, 'Ukraine, Russia, and US Policy', PONARS Policy Memo, no. 91, April 2001, https://www.gwu.edu/~ieresgwu/assets/docs/ponars/pm_0191.pdf.

79 James Goldgeier and Michael McFaul, *Power and Purpose: U.S. Policy toward Russia After the Cold War* (Washington DC: Brookings Institution Press, 2003), p. 118.

80 'BBC Breakfast with Frost, Interview: Vladimir Putin', 5 March 2000, http://news.bbc.co.uk/hi/english/static/audio_video/programmes/breakfast_with_frost/transcripts/putin5.mar.txt.

81 Robyn Dixon, 'With NATO Chief's Visit to Russia, a Thaw Begins', *Los Angeles Times*, 17 February 2000, http://articles.latimes.com/2000/feb/17/news/mn-65412.

82 Authors' interview with a former senior Russian official, May 2016.

83 Hill, *Russia, the Near Abroad, and the West*, p. 39.

84 Online records note expenditures on GUAM/GUUAM in fiscal years 2001 and 2002, without giving exact numbers. There is no annotation for 2003, but in fiscal year 2004 there are entries of US$250,000 through Department of State accounts and US$520,000 through the Department

of Homeland Security. The 2002 framework agreement can be found at http://guam-organization.org/en/node/461.

85 Hill, *Russia, the Near Abroad, and the West*, p. xii.

86 'Vystuplenie na konferentsii Memorial'nogo fonda Dzhavakharlala Neru', 3 December 2004, http://kremlin.ru/events/president/transcripts/22720.

Chapter Two

1 Besides the two small island nations of Malta and Cyprus, all the new EU members were either former Soviet republics (Estonia, Latvia and Lithuania), former communist states in East Central Europe (the Czech Republic, Hungary, Poland and Slovakia) or the Balkans (Slovenia, once a constituent republic of Yugoslavia). NATO took in Bulgaria, Estonia, Latvia, Lithuania, Romania, Slovakia and Slovenia in 2004. Bulgaria and Romania were to accede to the EU in 2007 and Croatia in the Balkans to NATO in 2009 and the EU in 2013.

2 See presentations by Minister of Defence Sergei Shoigu, Foreign Minister Sergei Lavrov and Chief of the General Staff Valerii Gerasimov at the 3rd annual Moscow Conference on International Security, available at http://mil.ru/mcis/2014.htm. For an English-language summary, see http://eng.mil.ru/files/MCIS_report_catalogue_final_ENG_21_10_preview.pdf.

3 Valerii Gerasimov, 'Tsennost' nauki v prognozirovanii', *Voenno-promyshlennyi kur'er*, 5 March 2013.

4 As Michael McFaul notes, the foreign democracy-promotion wings of both of the United States' national political parties were deeply involved in Ukrainian events in 2004: 'That there were purposive efforts by both IRI [the International Republican Institute] and NDI [the National Democratic Institute] to strengthen Our Ukraine's [Yushchenko's party] campaign abilities is without question.' Michael McFaul, 'Ukraine Imports Democracy: External Influences on the Orange Revolution', *International Security*, vol. 32, no. 2, Fall 2007, p. 74.

5 Lincoln A. Mitchell, *The Color Revolutions* (Philadelphia, PA: University of Pennsylvania Press, 2012), p. 86.

6 See Henry E. Hale, *Patronal Politics: Eurasian Regime Dynamics in Comparative Perspective* (Cambridge: Cambridge University Press, 2014).

7 It is conceivable that in Georgia the cosy relationship with the Bush administration actually encouraged nondemocratic behaviour, by leading Saakashvili to think he could mistreat local opponents without objection from external patrons.

8 See, for example, Nicolas Bouchet, 'Russia and the Democracy Rollback in Europe', The German Marshall Fund of the United States, 26 May 2016, http://www.gmfus.org/publications/russia-and-democracy-rollback-europe.

9 Timothy Colton, 'Sources and Limits of Russia's Influence in Post-Soviet Eurasia', paper presented at the Annual Meeting of the American Political Science Association, Seattle, WA, 3 September 2011, p. 11.

10 Nelli Babayan, 'The Return of the Empire? Russia's Counteraction to Transatlantic Democracy Promotion in Its Near Abroad', *Democratization*, vol. 22, no. 3, March 2015, pp. 438–58.

11 Andrei Kolesnikov, 'Obnimai, no proveryai', *Kommersant*, 21 March 2005.

12 'Nachalo vstrechi s prem'er-ministrom Ukrainy Yuliei Timoshenko', 19 March 2005, http://kremlin.ru/events/president/transcripts/22867.

13 'Commission Staff Working Paper – European Neighbourhood Policy – Country Report Ukraine {COM(2004)373 Final}', 12 May 2004, http://www.enpi-info.eu/library/content/ukraine-enp-country-report.

14 'Russia – Final Version of the Road Map on the Common Economic Space Agreed at the EU–Russia Summit on 10 May', 24 May 2005, http://www.enpi-info.eu/library/content/eu-russia-roadmap-common-economic-space.

15 Jonathan Stern, 'The Russian–Ukrainian Gas Crisis of January 2006', Oxford Institute for Energy Studies, 16 January 2006, p. 6.

16 Rilka Dragneva and Kataryna Wolczuk, *Ukraine Between the EU and Russia* (London: Palgrave Macmillan, 2015), p. 74.

17 James Sherr, *Hard Diplomacy and Soft Coercion: Russia's Influence Abroad* (London: Chatham House, 2013).

18 Marlene Laruelle, 'The "Russian World": Russia's Soft Power and Geopolitical Imagination', Center on Global Interests, May 2015; Sinikukka Saari, 'Russia's Post-Orange Revolution Strategies to Increase Its Influence in Former Soviet Republics: Public Diplomacy *Po Russkii*', *Europe–Asia Studies*, vol. 66, no. 1, January 2014, pp. 50–66.

19 Dick Cheney, *In My Time: A Personal and Political Memoir* (New York: Threshold Editions, 2012), p. 428.

20 Ronald Asmus, 'Redrawing (Again) the Map of Europe: A Strategy for Integrating Ukraine into the West', in Joerg Forbrig and Robin Shepherd (eds), *Ukraine after the Orange Revolution: Strengthening European and Transatlantic Commitments* (Washington DC: The German Marshall Fund of the United States, 2005), p. 90.

21 George W. Bush, *Decision Points* (New York: Broadway Books, 2011), p. 430.

22 'Cheney's Speech in Lithuania', 4 May 2006, http://www.nytimes.com/2006/05/04/world/europe/04cnd-cheney-text.html.

23 In 2006, NATO membership was broadly unpopular among Ukrainians, including in the traditionally pro-Western central and western regions, where 23% supported and 29% opposed, to say nothing of the south and east, traditionally more pro-Russian (7% support for NATO, 77% opposed). Kyiv International Institute of Sociology data cited in Valeriy Khmel'ko, 'Cherez shcho politykam vdayet'sya rozkolyuvaty Ukrayinu', *Dzerkalo tyzhnya*, 23 June 2006, http://gazeta.dt.ua/ARCHIVE/cherez_scho_politikam_vdaetsya_rozkolyuvati_ukrayinu.html.

24 'Ukraine on the Road to NATO: A Status Report', 14 February 2006, released by WikiLeaks as Cable 06KIEV604_a, https://wikileaks.org/plusd/cables/06KIEV604_a.html.

25 According to the US Department of State, at least US$2.5 million was spent on GUAM-related projects between the fiscal years 2004 and 2008. See US Government Assistance to and Cooperative Activities with Eurasia, http://www.state.gov/p/eur/rls/rpt/

c10250.htm.

26 The Russian peacekeepers in Abkhazia and South Ossetia, stationed there under the terms of the ceasefire agreements that ended the conflicts of the early 1990s, were thus not covered by the Istanbul Commitments and remained.

27 Some details may be found in 'A/S Fried-Poldir Araud on Iran, Kosovo, Georgia, Moldova/CFE, NATO Ministerial', 31 January 2007, released by WikiLeaks as Cable 07PARIS363_a, https://search.wikileaks.org/plusd/cables/07PARIS363_a.html; 'CFE: Germany Pushes for Being Forward-Leaning on A/CFE Ratification at Upcoming Extraordinary Conference', 4 June 2007, released by WikiLeaks as Cable 07BERLIN1107_a, https://search.wikileaks.org/plusd/cables/07BERLIN1107_a.html; 'November 7 HLTF and NRC-ACE Meetings at NATO', 28 November 2006, released by WikiLeaks as Cable 06USNATO687_a, https://search.wikileaks.org/plusd/cables/06USNATO687_a.html.

28 'Poslanie Federal'nomu Sobraniyu Rossiiskoi Federatsii', 26 April 2007, http://kremlin.ru/events/president/transcripts/24203.

29 It should be noted that the CFE treaty contains no suspension clause so the Russian move was of dubious legality.

30 'DFM Karasin on Ukraine, Georgia, Transnistria, Armenia and Belarus', 8 February 2008, released by WikiLeaks as Cable 08MOSCOW353_a, https://wikileaks.org/plusd/cables/08MOSCOW353_a.html.

31 Condoleezza Rice, *No Higher Honor: A Memoir of My Years in Washington* (New York: Broadway Paperbacks, 2012), p. 671.

32 Ronald D. Asmus, *A Little War That Shook the World: Georgia, Russia, and the Future of the West* (New York: Palgrave Macmillan, 2010), p. 117.

33 'Bush and Yushchenko Remark on Ukraine and Nato', *Washington Post*, 1 April 2008, http://www.washingtonpost.com/wp-dyn/content/article/2008/04/01/AR2008040101600.html.

34 Radek Sikorski, quoted in Rice, *No Higher Honor*, p. 674.

35 'Bucharest Summit Declaration', 3 April 2008, http://www.nato.int/cps/en/natolive/official_texts_8443.htm.

36 'Zayavlenie dlya pressy i otvety na voprosy zhurnalistov po itogam zasedaniya Soveta Rossiya–NATO', 4 April 2008, http://kremlin.ru/events/president/transcripts/24903.

37 Asmus, *A Little War That Shook the World*, p. 136.

38 'THE PRESIDENT IN EUROPE; Bush's Vision: "We Will Not Trade Away the Fate of Free European Peoples"', *New York Times*, 16 June 2001.

39 Moreover, the Yalta accords actually guaranteed Poland 'free elections of governments responsive to the will of the people', a provision, of course, which Stalin subsequently violated. See Conrad Black, 'The Yalta Myth', *National Interest*, May 2014, http://nationalinterest.org/article/the-yalta-myth-1052.

40 *Ibid.*

41 Asmus, *A Little War That Shook the World*, p. 146.

42 *Ibid.*, p. 149.

43 'Independent International Fact-Finding Mission on the Conflict in Georgia Report', September 2009, http://echr.coe.int/Documents/HUDOC_38263_08_Annexes_ENG.pdf.

44 'Ex-Ambassador of Georgia: Georgian Invasion to Abkhazia Was Prepared in April–May', *Caucasian Knot*, 25 November 2008, http://www. eng.kavkaz-uzel.eu/articles/8765/; International Crisis Group, 'Georgia and Russia: Clashing over Abkhazia', Europe Report no. 193, 5 June 2008.

45 According to Asmus, Saakashvili received reports on 7 August that Russia was massing troops on the border and even inside South Ossetia. Asmus, *A Little War That Shook the World*, p. 23. See also C.J. Chivers, 'Georgia Offers Fresh Evidence on War's Start', *New York Times*, 15 September 2008.

46 As Asmus writes, 'Throughout this period, Russian officials used both front and back diplomatic channels to tell their Western counterparts that their military steps were simply a deterrent to prevent the Georgians from acting rashly and attacking Abkhazia.' Asmus, *A Little War That Shook the World*, p. 145.

47 For example, Cheney called for granting a MAP in a speech in Italy in September 2008: 'At Bucharest only five months ago, we considered extending a Membership Action Plan to Georgia and Ukraine, but did not do so. But Allies agreed that those nations will be NATO members, and the time to begin their Membership Action Plans, I believe, has come.' 'Vice President's Remarks at the Ambrosetti Forum', 6 September 2008, http://georgewbush-whitehouse.archives.gov/news/releases/2008/09/20080906-1.html.

48 'Ukraine, MAP, and the Georgia–Russia Conflict', 14 August 2008, released by WikiLeaks as Cable 08USNATO290_a, https://wikileaks.org/plusd/cables/08USNATO290_a.html.

49 Dmitri Trenin, *Post-Imperium: A Eurasian Story* (Washington DC: Carnegie Endowment for International Peace, 2011), p. 98.

50 Asmus, *A Little War That Shook the World*, p. 186.

51 Joe Wood interview in Ben Smith, 'U.S. Pondered Military Use in Georgia', *Politico*, 3 February 2010, http://www.politico.com/story/2010/02/us-pondered-military-use-in-georgia-032487.

52 Dragneva and Wolczuk, *Ukraine Between the EU and Russia*, p. 4. The term 'normative power' was first used in Ian Manners, 'Normative Power Europe: A Contradiction in Terms?', *Journal of Common Market Studies*, vol. 40, no. 2, June 2002, pp. 235–58.

53 'Communication from the Commission to the Council and the European Parliament: Wider Europe – Neighbourhood: A New Framework for Relations with Our Eastern and Southern Neighbors {COM(2003) – 104 Final}', 11 March 2003, http://eeas.europa.eu/enp/pdf/pdf/com03_104_en.pdf.

54 Authors' interview with Javier Solana, June 2016.

55 Tom Casier, 'The Clash of Integration Processes? The Shadow Effect of the Enlarged EU on Its Eastern Neighbours', in Katlijn Malfliet, Lien Verpoest and Evgeny Vinokurov (eds), *The CIS, the EU and Russia: The Challenges of Integration* (Basingstoke: Palgrave Macmillan, 2007), p. 74.

56 Romano Prodi, 'Europe and the Mediterranean: Time for Action', Speech, Université Catholique de Louvain-la-Neuve, 26 November 2002, http://europa.eu/rapid/press-release_SPEECH-02-589_en.htm.

57 These are administered by the CIS Interstate Council for Standardization,

Metrology and Certification, which has a coordinating body in Minsk. Interestingly, all 12 non-Baltic former Soviet republics, including non-members of the CIS, are represented on the Council. See the Council's website for more information: http://www.easc.org.by/.

58 'Joint Statement on EU Enlargement and EU–Russia Relations' (European Union, 27 April 2004), http://www.enpi-info.eu/library/content/joint-statement-eu-enlargement-and-eu-russia-relations. See also Holger Moroff, 'EU Policies toward Russia', in Katlijn Malfliet, Lien Verpoest and Evgeny Vinokurov (eds), *The CIS, the EU, and Russia: The Challenges of Integration* (Basingstoke: Palgrave Macmillan, 2007).

59 'European Security Strategy: A Secure Europe in a Better World', 2009, p. 23, http://www.consilium.europa.eu/en/documents-publications/publications/2009/pdf/european-security-strategy-secure-europe-better-world/.

60 Authors' interview with Javier Solana.

61 Valentina Pop, 'EU Expanding Its "Sphere of Influence," Russia Says', *EUobserver*, 21 March 2009, https://euobserver.com/foreign/27827.

62 Constanze Stelzenmüller, 'Walk – But Learn to Chew the Gum Too. After the Russo–Georgian War of 2008: Transatlantic Approaches to a New Eastern Policy', paper presented at the 11th Annual Foreign Policy Conference of the Heinrich Böll Stiftung, Berlin, 27 September 2010, p. 10.

63 Andrei Zagorski, 'Eastern Partnership from the Russian Perspective', *Internationale Politik und Gesellschaft*, vol. 3, 2011, p. 46, http://library.fes.de/pdf-files/ipg/2011-3/05_zagorski.pdf.

64 'Government Statement Delivered by Chancellor Angela Merkel on the EU's Eastern Partnership Summit to Be Held on 28/29 November 2013 in Vilnius', 18 November 2013, https://www.bundeskanzlerin.de/ContentArchiv/EN/Archiv17/Regierungsrerkl%C3%A4rung/2013-11-18-merkel-oestl-partnerschaften.html.

65 The timing of the move was apparently due to a push from Kazakhstan's President Nazarbaev. It came as a surprise to many, including those officials negotiating Russia's WTO accession, who had to adjust that process to accommodate the new Customs Union.

66 See European Bank for Reconstruction and Development, 'Regional Trade Integration and Eurasian Economic Union', in *Transition Report 2012: Integration Across Borders*, 2012, pp. 62–79, http://tr.ebrd.com/tr12/images/downloads/TR12_EN_web_bookmarks3.pdf.

67 Vladimir Putin, 'Novyi integratsionnyi proekt dlya Evrazii — budushchee, kotoroe rozhdaetsya segodnya', *Izvestiya*, 3 October 2011.

68 Putin's conception of the Eurasian bloc forming an independent pole in global politics was remarkably similar to the way in which Russian officials talked about their aspirations for Russia.

69 Nursultan Nazarbaev, 'Evraziiskii Soyuz: ot idei k istorii budushchego', *Izvestiya*, 25 October 2011, http://izvestia.ru/news/504908.

70 Putin, 'Novyi integratsionnyi proekt dlya Evrazii'.

71 Denis Cenusa et al., 'Russia's Punitive Trade Policy Measures towards Ukraine, Moldova and Georgia', CEPS Working Document, Centre for European Policy Studies, September

2014, pp. 7–8.

72 See the draft foreign-policy strategy produced for Medvedev, as leaked to the press: 'O programme effektivnogo ispol'zovaniya na sistemnoi osnove vneshnepoliticheskikh faktorov v tselyakh dolgosrochnogo razvitiya Rossiiskoi Federatsii', https://www.hse.ru/data/2010/09/27/1223786940/Foreign_policy_for_modernisation_program.doc.

73 Michael McFaul, 'Assessing the "Reset": Past Progress, Future Steps', Presentation, Peterson Institute for International Economics, 15 April 2011, https://piie.com/sites/default/files/publications/papers/mcfaul20110415.pdf.

74 Michael McFaul, 'The Russian Economy and US–Russia Relations', Event Transcript, Peterson Institute for International Economics, 15 April 2011, https://piie.com/publications/papers/transcript-20110415mcfaul.pdf.

75 'Joint Statement of the Presidents of the United States and the Russian Federation in Connection with the Situation in the Kyrgyz Republic', 24 June 2010, https://www.whitehouse.gov/sites/default/files/us-russia_joint_statement_on_kyrgyzstan.pdf.

76 'NATO–Russia Council Joint Statement at the Meeting of the NATO–Russia Council Held in Lisbon on 20 November 2010', 20 November 2010, http://www.nato.int/cps/en/natohq/news_68871.htm.

77 Nikonov quoted in Gregory L. White, 'In Secret Report, Russia Shifts Westward', *Wall Street Journal*, 12 May 2010, http://www.wsj.com/articles/SB10001424052748703565804575238291897667152.

78 Samuel Charap and Mikhail Troitskiy, 'U.S.–Russia Relations in Post-Soviet Eurasia: Transcending the Zero-Sum Game', Working Group on the Future of US–Russia Relations, September 2011, p. 19, https://futureofusrussiarelations.files.wordpress.com/2013/01/us-russiafuture_working_group_paper_1.pdf.

79 'Vystuplenie na Konferentsii po voprosam mirovoi politiki', 8 October 2008, http://kremlin.ru/events/president/transcripts/1659.

80 'Stenograficheskii otchet o vstreche s uchastnikami mezhdunarodnogo kluba "Valdai"', 12 September 2008, http://kremlin.ru/events/president/transcripts/1383.

81 'Interv'yu Dmitriya Medvedeva rossiiskim telekanalam', 31 August 2008, http://kremlin.ru/events/president/news/1276.

82 'Remarks by Vice President Biden at 45th Munich Conference on Security Policy', 7 February 2009, https://www.whitehouse.gov/the-press-office/remarks-vice-president-biden-45th-munich-conference-security-policy.

83 'The Draft of the European Security Treaty', 29 November 2009, http://en.kremlin.ru/events/president/news/6152.

84 Hillary Rodham Clinton, 'Remarks on the Future of European Security', 29 January 2010, http://www.state.gov/secretary/20092013clinton/rm/2010/01/136273.htm.

85 'ASD/ISA Vershbow's September 30 Visit to Moscow: Bilateral Cooperation, Iran, Afghanistan, Missile Defense, Military/Defense Cooperation', released by WikiLeaks as Cable 09MOSCOW2529_a, https://wikileaks.org/plusd/cables/09MOSCOW2529_a.html.

86 State Department cable cited in Joshua Kucera, 'U.S. Blocking

NATO–CSTO Cooperation', *EurasiaNet*, 12 February 2011, http://www.eurasianet.org/node/62882.

[87] 'Memorandum, Meeting of Chancellor Angela Merkel and President Dmitri Medvedev on 4–5 June 2010 in Meseberg', 5 June 2010, http://www.russianmission.eu/sites/ default/files/user/files/2010-06-05-meseberg-memorandum.pdf. See also Philip Remler, 'Negotiation Gone Bad: Russia, Germany, and Crossed Communications', Carnegie Europe, 21 August 2013, http://carnegieeurope.eu/publications/?fa=52712.

Chapter Three

[1] Calculations by Pierre Noel, Senior Fellow for Economic and Energy Security, International Institute for Strategic Studies, shared with the authors.

[2] Natal'ya Grib and Oleg Gavrish, 'Ravnotrubie', *Kommersant Ukraina*, 14 May 2010, http://www.kommersant.ru/doc/1368732.

[3] Vera Sitnina, 'Tak rabotat' nel'zya, no pridetsya', *Vremya novostei*, 18 May 2010, http://www.vremya.ru/2010/83/4/253821.html.

[4] 'Predsedatel' Pravitel'stva Rossiiskoi Federatsii V.V.Putin vstretilsya s Prezidentom Ukrainy V.F.Yanukovichem', 5 March 2010, http://archive.government.ru/docs/9632/.

[5] See 'Rossiya rasschityvaet, chto Ukraina k 2015 godu voidet v Tamozhennyi soyuz', *RIA Novosti*, 9 December 2012, http://ria.ru/economy/20121209/914040052.html; Rilka Dragneva and Kataryna Wolczuk, *Ukraine Between the EU and Russia* (London: Palgrave Macmillan, 2015), p. 68.

[6] See, for example, Evraziiskii Bank Razvitiya, 'Ukraina i Tamozhennyi soyuz', 2012, http://www.eabr.org/general/upload/reports/Ukraina_doklad_rus.pdf.

[7] Valerii Kalnysh, 'Viktor Yanukovich reshil slozhit'sya c Rossiei', *Kommersant*, 8 April 2011, http://www.kommersant.ru/doc/1616528.

[8] Sergei Sidorenko, 'Tamozhennyi soyuz — eto tol'ko pervyi etap integratsii', *Kommersant*, 18 April 2011, http://www.kommersant.ru/doc/1623955.

[9] 'Posol Ukrainy v RF nazval usloviya vstupleniya v Tamozhennyi soyuz', *Zerkalo nedeli*, 13 November 2012, http://zn.ua/ECONOMICS/posol_ukrainy_v_rf_nazval_usloviya_vstupleniya_v_tamozhennyy_soyuz.html.

[10] After a deputy prime minister declared that Customs Union membership contravened Ukrainian law, then-prime minister Mykola Azarov publicly contradicted him during a visit to Moscow. See 'Azarov zaveril Rossiyu, chto ne schitaet chlenstvo Ukrainy v Tamozhennom soyuze nezakonnym', *Zerkalo nedeli*, 21 November 2012, http://zn.ua/ECONOMICS/azarov_zaveril_rossiyu,_chto_ne_schitaet_chlenstvo_ukrainy_v_tamozhennom_soyuze_nezakonnym.html.

[11] 'V Evrosoyuze zayavili, chto lyuboe uchastie Ukrainy v Tamozhennom soyuze nesovmestimo s dal'neishei

evrointegratsiei', *Zerkalo nedeli*, 25 December 2012, http://zn.ua/POLITICS/evrosoyuze_zayavili,_chto_lyuboe_uchastie_ukrainy_v_tamozhennom_soyuze_nesovmestimo_s_dalneyshey_evr.html.

12 'Vmesto pozdravleniya: Rossiya pred'yavila Ukraine tamozhenno-gazovyi ul'timatum', *NEWSru.com*, 2 January 2013, http://www.newsru.com/finance/02jan2013/rus_ukr.html.

13 Sergei Sidorenko and Andrei Kolesnikov, 'Mezhdu soyuzom i sovetom', *Kommersant Ukraina*, 30 May 2013, http://www.kommersant.ru/doc/2200231.

14 Roman Olearchyk, 'Russia Accused of Triggering Trade War with Ukraine', *Financial Times*, 15 August 2013, http://www.ft.com/cms/s/0/99068c0e-0595-11e3-8ed5-00144feab7de.html.

15 Just in case Kyiv misunderstood, Glaziev, by now a Kremlin adviser to the president, spelled it out in a statement to the press. See Sergei Smirnov, 'Rossiya ob"yasnila uzhestochenie tamozhennogo rezhima s Ukrainoi', *Vedomosti*, 18 August 2013, https://www.vedomosti.ru/politics/articles/2013/08/18/rossijskie-vlasti-obyasnili-za-tamozhne.

16 Mykola Ryzhenkov, Veronika Movchan and Ricardo Giucci, 'Impact Assessment of a Possible Change in Russia's Trade Regime Vis-a-Vis Ukraine', Institute for Economic Research and Policy Consulting/German Advisory Group, November 2013, http://www.beratergruppe-ukraine.de/download/PolicyBriefings/2013/PB_04_2013_en.pdf.

17 'Zasedanie mezhdunarodnogo diskussionnogo kluba "Valdai"', 19 September 2013, http://kremlin.ru/events/president/news/19243.

18 Christiane Hoffmann et al., 'Summit of Failure: How the EU Lost Russia over Ukraine, Part 2: Four Thousand Deaths and an Eastern Ukraine Gripped by War', *Spiegel Online*, 24 November 2014, http://www.spiegel.de/international/europe/war-in-ukraine-a-result-of-misunderstandings-between-europe-and-russia-a-1004706-2.html.

19 *Ibid.*

20 'Zayavleniya dlya pressy po okonchanii zasedaniya Rossiisko-Ukrainskoi mezhgosudarstvennoi komissii', 17 December 2013, http://kremlin.ru/events/president/transcripts/19854.

21 Yanukovych allegedly met secretly with Putin three times in October–November in order to agree the details of the financial-support package, while still sending positive signals to the EU about Vilnius. See Sonya Koshkina, *Maidan: Nerasskazannaya istoriya* (Kyiv: Brait Star, 2015), p. 25.

22 International Foundation for Electoral Systems, 'IFES Public Opinion in Ukraine 2013: Key Findings', December 2013, http://pdf.usaid.gov/pdf_docs/pnaec646.pdf.

23 'Ukraine Crisis: Transcript of Leaked Nuland–Pyatt Call', BBC News, 7 February 2014, http://www.bbc.com/news/world-europe-26079957.

24 Koshkina, *Maidan*, p. 165; 'EU Mulls Aid Package for Crisis-Ridden Ukraine', Associated Press, 3 February 2014, http://bigstory.ap.org/article/eu-mulls-aid-package-crisis-ridden-ukraine.

25 The agreement is available at http://zn.ua/POLITICS/obnarodovan-tekst-soglasheniya-ob-uregulirovanii-krizisa-v-ukraine-139374_.html.

26 Mick Krever, 'Putin Phone Call

Convinced Yanukovych to Change Attitude, Says Polish Foreign Minister', Amanpour Blog, CNN, 26 February 2014, http://amanpour.blogs.cnn.com/2014/02/26/vladimir-putin-viktor-yanukovych-radoslaw-sikorski-ukraine-poland-russia/.

27 'Readout of President Obama's Call with President Putin', 21 February 2014, https://www.whitehouse.gov/the-press-office/2014/02/21/readout-president-obama-s-call-president-putin.

28 Keith Darden, 'How to Save Ukraine: Why Russia is Not the Real Problem', Foreign Affairs, 14 April 2014, https://www.foreignaffairs.com/articles/russian-federation/2014-04-14/how-save-ukraine.

29 'Secretary Kerry Speaks With Russian Foreign Minister Lavrov About the Situation in Ukraine', 23 February 2014, https://blogs.state.gov/stories/2014/02/23/secretary-kerry-speaks-russian-foreign-minister-lavrov-about-situation-ukraine.

30 'Remarks by EU High Representative Catherine Ashton at the End of Her Visit to Ukraine', 25 February 2014, http://www.eeas.europa.eu/statements/docs/2014/140225_01_en.pdf.

31 Comments by McFaul during a talk at the German Marshall Fund of the United States in Washington DC on 9 June 2016.

32 Lukas I. Alpert, 'Russia's Medvedev Calls Ukraine a Possible Threat', Wall Street Journal, 24 February 2014, http://www.wsj.com/articles/SB10001424052702304834704579402922004993600; 'Vystuplenie i otvety na voprosy SMI', 25 February 2014, http://www.mid.ru/ru/press_service/minister_speeches/-/asset_publisher/7OvQR5KJWVmR/content/id/73790?p_p_id=101_

INSTANCE_7OvQR5KJWVmR&_101_INSTANCE_7OvQR5KJWVmR_languageId=ru_RU.

33 For a full timeline of events leading up to and following the annexation of Crimea, see Colby Howard and Ruslan Pukhov (eds), Brothers Armed: Military Aspects of the Crisis in Ukraine (Minneapolis, MN: East View Press, 2015), pp. 209–13.

34 'Stenohrama zasidannya Rady natsional'noyi bezpeky i oborony Ukrayiny vid 28 lyutoho 2014 roku', 28 February 2014, http://komnbo.rada.gov.ua/komnbo/control/uk/publish/article?art_id=53495&cat_id=44731.

35 Polling data in Mezhdunarodnyi diskussionyi klub Valdai, 'Sovremennaya rossiiskaya identichnost': izmereniya, vyzovy, otvety', September 2013, http://vid-1.rian.ru/ig/valdai/Russian_Identity_2013_rus.pdf.

36 See Putin's remarks during a press conference that day: 'Vladimir Putin otvetil na voprosy zhurnalistov o situatsii na Ukraine', 4 March 2014, http://kremlin.ru/events/president/news/20366.

37 'Readout of the President's Call with President Putin', 16 March 2014, https://www.whitehouse.gov/the-press-office/2014/03/16/readout-president-s-call-president-putin.

38 'Obrashchenie Prezidenta Rossiiskoi Federatsii', 18 March 2014, http://kremlin.ru/events/president/news/20603.

39 Valerii Shiryaev, 'Vosem' zhenshchin v dekretnom otpuske, moryak-geroi i real'naya agentura rossiiskikh spetssluzhb. Kogo vklyuchili v spisok predatelei Ukrainy?', Novaya gazeta, 29 March 2016, http://www.novayagazeta.ru/politics/72441.html.

40 The Russian Ministry of Foreign Affairs published the proposal online two days later: 'Zayavlenie MID Rossii o Gruppe podderzhki dlya Ukrainy', 17 March 2014, http://archive.mid.ru//brp_4.nsf/newsline/49766426492B6 E9644257C9E0036B79A. Referred to hereafter as the '15 March document' since that was when it was presented to the US secretary of state.

41 'Pryamaya liniya s Vladimirom Putinym', 17 April 2014, http://kremlin.ru/events/president/news/20796. As it happens, his claim about the Soviet government's decisions in the 1920s was false.

42 'Press Release: IMF Executive Board Approves 2-Year US$17.01 Billion Stand-By Arrangement for Ukraine, US$3.19 Billion for Immediate Disbursement', 30 April 2014, https://www.imf.org/external/np/sec/pr/2014/pr14189.htm. Less than a year later, the IMF announced a slightly larger programme and also lengthened the programme timeline. 'Press Release: IMF Executive Board Approves 4-Year US$17.5 Billion Extended Fund Facility for Ukraine, US$5 Billion for Immediate Disbursement', 11 March 2015, https://www.imf.org/external/np/sec/pr/2015/pr15107.htm.

43 Japan also instituted sanctions, but they were far less potent.

44 'The Hague Declaration Following the G7 Meeting on 24 March', 24 March 2014, http://europa.eu/rapid/press-release_STATEMENT-14-82_en.htm.

45 Dual-use items constituted a sizeable percentage of US exports to Russia. In 2013, the Department of Commerce approved 1,832 licence applications for dual-use exports to Russia, which together amounted to US$1.5 billion of exports, or 14.4% of total US exports to Russia. See Alan M. Dunn and Jennifer M. Smith, 'Russia and Ukraine Update: The U.S. Has Stopped Issuing of Export Licenses to Russia and the U.S., Canada, and the EU Have Expanded Sanctions, But Loan Guarantees to Ukraine Provide Opportunities for U.S. Businesses', Stewart and Stewart, 16 April 2014, http://www.stewartlaw.com/Article/ViewArticle/997.

46 'Remarks by President Obama and German Chancellor Merkel in Joint Press Conference', 2 May 2014, https://www.whitehouse.gov/the-press-office/2014/05/02/remarks-president-obama-and-german-chancellor-merkel-joint-press-confere.

47 'Ukraine – Countering Russian Intervention and Supporting a Democratic State', 6 May 2014, http://www.state.gov/p/eur/rls/rm/2014/may/225674.htm.

48 Authors' correspondence with Sergei Karaganov, September 2016.

49 'Announcement of Expanded Treasury Sanctions within the Russian Financial Services, Energy and Defense or Related Materiel Sectors', 12 September 2014, https://www.treasury.gov/press-center/press-releases/Pages/jl2629.aspx.

50 'Geneva Statement on Ukraine', 17 April 2014, http://www.state.gov/r/pa/prs/ps/2014/04/224957.htm.

51 'Statement by the President on Ukraine', 29 July 2014, https://www.whitehouse.gov/the-press-office/2014/07/29/statement-president-ukraine.

52 'Lavrov to RT: Americans Are "Running the Show" in Ukraine', RT, 23 April 2014, https://www.rt.com/shows/sophieco/154364-lavrov-ukraine-standoff-sophieco/.

53 Interview with senior US official, Washington DC, June 2014.

54 See Neil Buckley et al., 'Battle for Ukraine: How a Diplomatic Success Unravelled', *Financial Times*, 3 February 2015, http://www.ft.com/intl/cms/s/2/7cfc8ac6-ab17-11e4-91d2-00144feab7de.html.

55 Quoted in Neil Buckley et al., 'Battle for Ukraine: How the West Lost Putin', *Financial Times*, 2 February 2015, http://www.ft.com/cms/s/2/e3ace220-a252-11e4-9630-00144feab7de.html.

56 Quoted in Buckley et al., 'Battle for Ukraine: How a Diplomatic Success Unravelled'.

57 Andrew Roth, 'Putin Tells European Official That He Could "Take Kiev in Two Weeks"', *New York Times*, 2 September 2014, http://www.nytimes.com/2014/09/03/world/europe/ukraine-crisis.html.

58 Quoted in Buckley et al., 'Battle for Ukraine: How the West Lost Putin'.

59 Office of the UN High Commissioner for Human Rights, 'Protracted Conflict in Eastern Ukraine Continues to Take Heavy Toll on Civilians', 8 October 2014, http://www.ohchr.org/en/NewsEvents/Pages/DisplayNews.aspx?NewsID=15143&LangID=E.

60 UN Office for the Coordination of Humanitarian Affairs, 'Ukraine: Situation Report No. 29 as of 27 February 2015', 27 February 2015, http://reliefweb.int/sites/reliefweb.int/files/resources/Sitrep%20%2329%20FINAL_1.pdf.

61 In the separatists' proposal, Ukraine would be transformed from its current unitary state into a highly asymmetrical confederation: the central government would be forced to negotiate agreements on all elements of public life with DNR/LNR, while the rest of the country would remain under the current system. See 'Popravki DNR i LNR v Konstitutsiyu Ukrainy', 13 March 2015, http://dan-news.info/official/popravki-dnr-i-lnr-v-konstituciyu-ukrainy.html.

62 See, for example, Andrew E. Kramer, 'Ex-Professor Upsets Ukraine Politics, and Russia Peace Accord', *New York Times*, 18 March 2016, http://www.nytimes.com/2016/03/19/world/europe/ukraine-oksana-syroyid.html; 'Seichas my mozhem tol'ko derzhat' oboronu — Lutsenko', 24 kanal, 7 September 2014, http://24tv.ua/ru/seychas_mi_mozhem_tolko_derzhat_oboronu__lutsenko_n482512; Vladimir Gorbulin, 'Est' li zhizn' posle Minska?', *Zerkalo nedeli*, 12 February 2016, http://gazeta.zn.ua/internal/est-li-zhizn-posle-minska-razmyshleniya-o-neizbezhnosti-neobhodimyh-izmeneniy-_.html.

63 Vladimir Lukin interview in Marat Gel'man, 'Voennyi plan Kremlya', *Novoe vremya*, 30 August 2014, http://nv.ua/opinion/gelman/voennyy-plan-kremlya--9686.html. Lukin, the former ambassador to the United States quoted in Chapter 1, was Putin's representative at the talks that produced the 21 February agreement.

64 Neil Buckley et al., Unpublished reporting provided to the authors, February 2015.

65 'Vystuplenie na vstreche glav gosudarstv Tamozhennogo soyuza s Prezidentom Ukrainy i predstavitelyami Evropeiskogo soyuza', 26 August 2014, http://kremlin.ru/events/president/transcripts/46494.

66 Buckley et al., Unpublished reporting provided to the authors.

67 As one EU delegate involved in the talks said, 'This whole concern about the [tariff lines] was always political, it wasn't commercial.' Quoted in *Ibid*.

68 Reporting by the *Financial Times*. Buckley et al., 'Battle for Ukraine: How a Diplomatic Success Unravelled'; Buckley et al., Unpublished reporting provided to the authors.

69 For example, Russia would have allowed Ukraine to use non-EU (i.e., CIS) plant-safety standards in its trade with non-EU countries. Ukraine would retain the policymaking competences that the DCFTA cedes to Brussels. EEU members would be consulted on any major changes to Ukrainian legislation stemming from the EU approximation process, and the EU and Ukraine would commit not to adopt laws that negatively affect Ukraine's trade with EEU members. And all 2,340 tariff lines that Putin referred to were listed. See 'Predlozheniya rossiiskoi storony po vneseniyu popravok Soglasheniya ob assotsiatsii mezhdu ES i gosudarstvami – chlenami ES s odnoi storony i Ukrainoi s drugoi storony v tselyakh minimizatsii riskov, voznikayushchikh ot vstupleniya v silu ukazannogo soglasheniya', http://zn.ua/static/file/russian_proposal.pdf.

70 Buckley et al., Unpublished reporting provided to the authors.

71 Peter Spiegel, 'Putin Demands Reopening of EU Trade Pact with Ukraine', *Financial Times*, 25 September 2014, http://www.ft.com/cms/s/0/a4de51ae-44ca-11e4-9a5a-00144feabdco.html.

72 Robin Emmott, 'Putin Warns Ukraine against Implementing EU Deal – Letter', Reuters, 23 September 2014, http://www.reuters.com/article/us-ukraine-crisis-trade-idUSKCN0HI1T820140923.

73 'Godovoi raund peregovorov RF-ES-Ukraina po torgovle okonchilsya nichem', TASS, 21 December 2015, http://tass.ru/ekonomika/2546713; European Commission, 'No Outcome Reached at the Final Trilateral Ministerial Meeting on the EU–Ukraine Deep and Comprehensive Free Trade Area', 21 December 2015, http://europa.eu/rapid/press-release_IP-15-6389_en.htm; European Commission, 'Trilateral Talks on EU–Ukraine DCFTA: Distinguishing between Myths & Reality', December 2015, http://trade.ec.europa.eu/doclib/docs/2015/december/tradoc_154127.pdf; 'Putin rasskazal o "ne ochen' evropeiskom" shage delegatsii ES v Bryussele', *lenta.ru*, 22 December 2015, https://lenta.ru/news/2015/12/22/putin/.

74 As Dragneva and Wolzcuk write, 'Its objections regarding the incompatibility of integration rules and processes seem spurious, and instead come across as an overt attempt to delineate its sphere of influence, in turn negating the sovereign right of Ukraine to leave this sphere and pursue economic integration with the EU.' Dragneva and Wolczuk, *Ukraine Between the EU and Russia*, p. 117.

Chapter Four

1 Only time will tell if this loss is irreparable, but it is obvious that Russia under its current rulers, and quite likely under their successors, will be loath to give this territory back. It cannot be recovered by force of arms. It is doubtful if the population would cooperate in any reversal of status, barring a drastic change in circumstances.

2 For example, Sberbank, Russia's omnipresent state-controlled savings bank, with offices in the West, has not operated branches in Crimea since the annexation for fear of running afoul of the sanctions. See 'Sberbank nazval rabotu v Krymu nepozvolitel'noi dlya sebya', Interfax, 29 May 2015, http://www.interfax.ru/business/444505.

3 In a telltale sign that not all Crimeans are thrilled with their new situation, a retiree berated Dmitry Medvedev, now prime minister of Russia, about her inadequate pension. With the cameras rolling, the most he could offer in response was, 'There's no money, but you hang in there!'

4 Organization for Security and Co-operation in Europe, Office for Democratic Institutions and Human Rights and High Commissioner on National Minorities, 'Report of the Human Rights Assessment Mission on Crimea (6–18 July 2015)', 17 September 2015, http://www.osce.org/odihr/180596?download=true.

5 Amnesty International, 'Ukraine: One Year On: Violations of the Rights to Freedom of Expression, Assembly and Association in Crimea', 18 March 2015, https://www.amnesty.org/en/documents/EUR50/1129/2015/en/.

6 Data from International Organization for Migration (May 2016) and UN High Commissioner for Refugees (June 2016), respectively. See International Organization for Migration, 'IOM Assistance to IDPs and Conflict-Affected Population in Ukraine', 19 May 2016, http://www.iom.org.ua/sites/default/files/general_map_eng_05-2016.png; UN High Commissioner for Refugees, 'Ukraine: UNHCR Operational Update, 14 May–10 June 2016', http://reliefweb.int/sites/reliefweb.int/files/resources/UNHCR%20Operational%20Update%20on%20the%20Ukraine%20Situation%20-%2014MAY-10JUN16.pdf.

7 Human Rights Watch and Amnesty International, '"You Don't Exist": Arbitrary Detentions, Forced Disappearances, and Torture in Eastern Ukraine', 21 July 2016, https://www.hrw.org/report/2016/07/21/you-dont-exist/arbitrary-detentions-enforced-disappearances-and-torture-eastern.

8 Office of the UN High Commissioner for Human Rights, 'Report on the Human Rights Situation in Ukraine 16 November 2015 to 15 February 2016', 3 March 2016, http://www.ohchr.org/Documents/Countries/UA/Ukraine_13th_HRMMU_Report_3March2016.pdf.

9 Office of the UN High Commissioner for Human Rights, 'Report on the Human Rights Situation in Ukraine 16 February to 15 May 2016', 3 June 2016, http://www.ohchr.org/Documents/Countries/UA/Ukraine_14th_HRMMU_Report.pdf.

10 Semen Dobryi and Vladimir Dergachev, 'Shla by lesom vasha

DNR – valyu v Rossiyu', *Gazeta.ru*, 16 October 2015, http://www.gazeta.ru/politics/2015/10/14_a_7820639.shtml.

11 Office of the UN High Commissioner for Human Rights, 'Report on the Human Rights Situation in Ukraine 16 February to 15 May 2016'.

12 Michael Bird, Lina Vdovii and Yana Tkachenko, 'The Donbass Paradox', The Black Sea, http://www.theblacksea.eu/donbass/.

13 Andrei Revenko, 'Kak my zhivem: udruchayushchie itogi 2015-go i perspektivy 2016-go', *Zerkalo nedeli*, 16 July 2016, http://gazeta.zn.ua/macrolevel/kak-my-zhivem-udruchayuschie-itogi-2015-go-i-perspektivy-2016-go-_.html.

14 Zach Bikus, 'Ukrainians' Life Ratings Sank to New Lows in 2015', Gallup, 4 January 2016, http://www.gallup.com/poll/187985/ukrainians-life-ratings-sank-new-lows-2015.aspx.

15 Calculations provided to the authors by Pierre Noel, Senior Fellow for Economic and Energy Security, International Institute for Strategic Studies. See also Simon Pirani, 'Ukraine's Imports of Russian Gas: How a Deal Might Be Reached', Oxford Institute for Energy Studies, July 2014, p. 4, https://www.oxfordenergy.org/wpcms/wp-content/uploads/2014/07/Ukraines-imports-of-Russian-gas-how-a-deal-might-be-reached.pdf.

16 World Trade Organization, 'Trade Policy Review Report by Ukraine', 15 March 2016, p. 10, https://www.wto.org/english/tratop_e/tpr_e/g334_e.pdf.

17 L.M. Grigor'ev, A.V. Golyashev and E.V. Buryak, 'Sotsial'no-ekonomicheskii krizis na Ukraine', Analytical Center for the Government of the Russian Federation Working Paper, September 2014, p. 26, http://ac.gov.ru/files/publication/a/3586.pdf.

18 UNITER, 'Corruption in Ukraine: Comparative Analysis of Nationwide Surveys of 2007, 2009, 2011 and 2015', April 2016; Julie Ray, 'Ukrainians Disillusioned With Leadership', Gallup, 23 December 2015, http://www.gallup.com/poll/187931/ukrainians-disillusioned-leadership.aspx.

19 Survey conducted by the Kyiv International Institute of Sociology, http://kiis.com.ua/?lang=ukr&cat=reports&id=231&page=1&y=2014&m=2.

20 Tom Parfitt, 'Ukraine Crisis: The Neo-Nazi Brigade Fighting Pro-Russian Separatists', *Telegraph*, 11 August 2014, http://www.telegraph.co.uk/news/worldnews/europe/ukraine/11025137/Ukraine-crisis-the-neo-Nazi-brigade-fighting-pro-Russian-separatists.html.

21 Calculations by Keith Darden, Associate Professor, School of International Service, American University, shared with the authors.

22 On the rubbish bins, see Roland Oliphant, 'Up to a Dozen Ukraine Officials Dumped in Wheelie Bins', *Telegraph*, 7 October 2014, http://www.telegraph.co.uk/news/worldnews/europe/ukraine/11145381/Up-to-a-dozen-Ukraine-officials-dumped-in-wheelie-bins.html.

23 Keith Gessen, 'Why Not Kill Them All?', *London Review of Books*, vol. 36, no. 17, 11 September 2014.

24 'Ukraine's Poroshenko: "New Russia" Is like "Mordor"', BBC News, 24 August 2015, http://www.bbc.com/news/world-europe-34037743.

25 GDP growth was negative for at least six consecutive quarters from Q3 2014 to Q4 2015. (2016 quarter-on-quarter data is unavailable at the time of writing.) During the 1998 crisis, there

were three negative quarters, and four in the global financial crisis of 2008–09.

26 See World Bank, 'Global Economic Prospects: Divergences and Risks', June 2016, p. 4, http://pubdocs.worldbank. org/en/842861463605615468/Global-Economic-Prospects-June-2016-Divergences-and-risks.pdf.

27 Konstantin Kholodilin and Aleksei Netšunajev, 'Crimea and Punishment: The Impact of Sanctions on Russian and European Economies', Discussion Papers, German Institute for Economic Research, 2016, https://www.diw. de/documents/publikationen/73/ diw_01.c.530645.de/dp1569.pdf. See also Christian Dreger et al., 'The Ruble between the Hammer and the Anvil: Oil Prices and Economic Sanctions', Discussion Papers, German Institute for Economic Research, 2015, https://www.diw.de/documents/ publikationen/73/diw_01.c.507887.de/ dp1488.pdf.

28 See World Bank, 'The Dawn of a New Economic Era?', Russia Economic Report, April 2015, pp. 33–42, https:// www.worldbank.org/content/dam/ Worldbank/document/eca/russia/ rer33-eng.pdf.

29 Polling conducted by the Levada Center, http://www.levada.ru/eng/ indexes-0.

30 See Mikhail Dmitriev, 'Between the Crimea and the Crisis: Attitude Change of Russians and Its Political Implications', Presentation, Center for Strategic and International Studies, 28 April 2015, pp. 16–26, https://csis-prod.s3.amazonaws.com/s3fs-public/ legacy_files/files/attachments/150428_ Dmitriev.pdf.

31 See, for example, Adrian Chen, 'The Agency', New York Times Magazine, 2 June 2015, http://www.nytimes. com/2015/06/07/magazine/the-agency. html.

32 Once the Russian military became more directly involved in the fighting in the Donbas, these nationalist volunteers were pushed out of the limelight. Those who resisted Moscow's effort to impose control ended up in a basement prison or, in some cases, dead; most returned to Russia. Some became outspoken critics of what they saw as feckless government policy.

33 Federal Ministry of Defence, 'White Paper on German Security Policy and the Future of the Bundeswehr', 13 July 2016, p. 32, https://www. bmvg.de/resource/resource/ MzEzNTM4MmUzMzMyMmUz MTM1MzMyZTM2MzIzMD MwMzAzMDMwMzAzMD Y5NzE3MzM1MzEzEzOTMy NmUyMDIwMjAyMDIw/2016%20 White%20Paper.pdf.

34 See Samuel Charap and Jeremy Shapiro, 'Consequences of a New Cold War', Survival: Global Politics and Strategy, vol. 57, no. 2, April–May 2015, pp. 37–46.

35 It would take some time to compensate for the post-1991 drawdown of Russian forces in its western quadrant. Compared with Russia's other frontiers, the western remains less heavily guarded.

36 On support for eurosceptical parties, see Suzanne Daley and Maïa de la Baume, 'French Far Right Gets Helping Hand With Russian Loan', New York Times, 1 December 2014, http://www. nytimes.com/2014/12/02/world/ europe/french-far-right-gets-helping-hand-with-russian-loan-.html.

37 'Remarks Previewing the FY 2017 Defense Budget', 2 February 2016, http://www.defense.gov/News/

Speeches/Speech-View/Article/648466/
remarks-previewing-the-fy-2017-
defense-budget.

38 Matthieu Crozet and Julian Hinz,
'Collateral Damage: The Impact of
the Russia Sanctions on Sanctioning
Countries' Exports', CEPII Working
Paper, Centre d'Etudes Prospectives
et d'Informations Internationales, June
2016, http://www.cepii.fr/PDF_PUB/
wp/2016/wp2016-16.pdf.

39 Ronald D. Asmus, *A Little War That
Shook the World: Georgia, Russia, and the
Future of the West* (New York: Palgrave
Macmillan, 2010), p. 71.

40 See Henry E. Hale, *Patronal Politics:
Eurasian Regime Dynamics in
Comparative Perspective* (Cambridge:
Cambridge University Press, 2014).

41 The five Central Asian countries have
more virulent strains of the same
pathologies.

42 Joel Hellman, 'Winners Take All:
The Politics of Partial Reform in
Postcommunist Transitions', *World
Politics*, vol. 50, no. 2, January 1998, pp.
203–34.

43 *Ibid.*, p. 233.

44 The EU, the World Bank and the
IMF froze financial aid to Moldova
in 2015 following revelations about
a bank-fraud scheme in which
private financiers and public officials
(including the prime minister)
embezzled more than US$1 billion,
or 12% of Moldova's GDP. Transfers
already authorised were not affected.
The EU's ambassador to Chisinau was
quoted in 2015 as saying he was baffled
by 'how it is possible to steal so much
money from a small country' (quoted in
Andrew Higgins, 'Moldova, Hunting
for Missing Millions, Finds Only Ash',
New York Times, 4 June 2015, http://
www.nytimes.com/2015/06/05/world/

europe/moldova-bank-theft.html).
Nevertheless, as of September 2016 the
EU had reopened the taps. See Cristi
Vlas, 'EU Commissioner Johannes
Hahn Visits Moldova, Brings a €15
Million Assistance Program for Public
Administration Reform', moldova.
org, 26 September 2016, http://www.
moldova.org/en/eu-commissioner-
johannes-hahn-visits-moldova-brings-
e15-million-assistance-program-
public-administration/.

45 International Foundation for Electoral
Systems, 'Ukraine 2013 Public Opinion
Poll Shows Dissatisfaction with Socio-
Political Conditions', 5 December
2013, http://www.ifes.org/news/
ukraine-2013-public-opinion-poll-
shows-dissastisfaction-socio-political-
conditions.

46 See polling in Steven Kull and Clay
Ramsay, 'The Ukrainian People on the
Current Crisis', Public Consultation
Program at the Center for International
and Security Studies at the University
of Maryland Report, March 2015, http://
www.cissm.umd.edu/publications/
ukrainian-people-current-crisis.

47 For evidence from 2014, see Gerard
Toal and John O'Loughlin, 'How
People in South Ossetia, Abkhazia and
Transnistria Feel about Annexation
by Russia', Washington Post Monkey
Cage Blog, 20 March 2014, https://www.
washingtonpost.com/news/monkey-
cage/wp/2014/03/20/how-people-in-
south-ossetia-abkhazia-and-transnistria-
feel-about-annexation-by-russia/.

48 International Republican Institute,
'Public Opinion Survey Residents
of Moldova, September 29–October
21, 2015', http://www.iri.org/sites/
default/files/wysiwyg/2015-11-09_
survey_of_moldovan_public_opinion_
september_29-october_21_2015.pdf.

[49] According to a disputed plebiscite conducted in February 2014, more than 98% of the Gagauz supported joining the Customs Union. See 'TsIK Gagauzii obnarodoval okonchatel'nye itogi referenduma o budushchei sud'be avtonomii', TASS, 5 February 2014, http://tass.ru/mezhdunarodnaya-panorama/940951.

[50] In a 2016 poll, 79% of Georgians favoured NATO membership and 85% membership of the EU. See International Republican Institute, 'Public Opinion Survey Residents of Georgia, March–April 2016', http://www.iri.org/sites/default/files/wysiwyg/georgia_2016.pdf.

[51] Toal and O'Loughlin, 'How People in South Ossetia, Abkhazia and Transnistria Feel about Annexation by Russia'.

[52] Human Rights Watch, 'Crossing the Line: Georgia's Violent Dispersal of Protestors and Raid on Imedi Television', 19 December 2007, https://www.hrw.org/report/2007/12/19/crossing-line/georgias-violent-dispersal-protestors-and-raid-imedi-television.

[53] Nelli Babayan, 'The In-Betweeners: The Eastern Partnership Countries and the Russia–West Conflict', 2015–16 Paper Series, Transatlantic Academy, April 2016, p. 1, http://www.gmfus.org/file/8150/download.

[54] EU officials cited in *Ibid.*, p. 13.

[55] As one European diplomat put it, '[Poroshenko] knows perfectly well that we cannot allow Ukraine to fail, that we have invested a lot in this country, and we need to have Ukraine as a success story. And he is abusing that knowledge. It is infuriating.' Quoted in Joshua Yaffa, 'Reforming Ukraine after the Revolution', *New Yorker*, 5 September 2016, http://www.newyorker.com/magazine/2016/09/05/reforming-ukraine-after-maidan.

[56] The Russian representative, Sergei Karaganov of the Higher School of Economics in Moscow, found it necessary to insert a 'letter of disagreement' into the document, in which he said he took issue with 24 of the points raised by Western members. The report, 'Back to Diplomacy', can be found at http://www.osce.org/networks/205846?download=true.

[57] This pattern, to be sure, applies more strictly to economic integration than to collective-security groupings.

[58] The ever-increasing economic role of China in post-Soviet Eurasia implies that the Russia–West binary of external patrons is already a thing of the past. We are grateful to Fyodor Lukyanov, Chairman of the Moscow-based Council on Foreign and Defence Policy, for this point.

[59] Hiski Haukkala, 'A Perfect Storm; Or What Went Wrong and What Went Right for the EU in Ukraine', *Europe–Asia Studies*, vol. 68, no. 4, June 2016, pp. 653–64.

[60] Charles A. Kupchan, *The End of the American Era: U.S. Foreign Policy and the Geopolitics of the Twenty-First Century* (New York: Random House, 2007), p. 14.

[61] This section draws on Samuel Charap and Jeremy Shapiro, 'US–Russian Relations: The Middle Cannot Hold', *Bulletin of the Atomic Scientists*, vol. 72, no. 3, April 2016, pp. 150–5.

[62] We should recall that the US policy of non-recognition of the Soviet occupation of the Baltic states did not prevent the agreement from going forward.

INDEX